Contents

Printing

by Michelle Powell

Printing is a process that involves making marks and reproducing those marks again and again. The marks can be shapes, patterns, pictures or words. Even a footprint in the snow is a basic form of printing.

The need for printing grew out of the need for written communication. Over five-and-a-half thousand years ago, the first writing appeared in Egypt as groups of symbols in clay tablets. As writing developed it was used to record events and re-tell stories. The ancient Egyptians wrote in pictures called hieroglyphics – one picture would represent a whole word or just part of a word. The Greeks, Romans, Vikings and other civilizations all had their own way of writing.

In the ninth century AD, the Chinese developed a method of printing using a carved wooden seal. They used this print to stamp official documents. Later, they produced carved wooden blocks to represent characters. The carved eraser stamps used in the dominoes project on pages 18–19 are made in a similar way.

Traditional printing methods are still used today. In this section I have looked at a variety of different techniques for making prints. The beauty of printing rather than drawing or painting, is that you can reproduce the same image over and over again, using the same printing block, tool or stamp. In this way you can quickly create a very detailed design with lots of repetition, or you can print on many items. This makes printing the perfect technique if you want to make lots of greetings cards for your friends, print up items to decorate your bedroom, or make unusual gifts for your family.

The first projects in the section use natural and man-made objects for printing. When you start looking for things to print with, you will soon discover that hundreds of different items are suitable. Cotton reels, scouring pads, bubblewrap, corrugated card, pen lids, corks and leaves can all be used to create interesting patterns and shapes.

I have also included projects which show different ways of creating printing blocks. You can use polystyrene, erasers, potatoes, string, foam and even pipe cleaners to make a fantastic range of designs. There are patterns at the end of the section that you can work from, or you can use your own drawings and designs to create unique prints.

Printing enables you to decorate many different things, and with a little experience you will soon be creating printed masterpieces of your own.

The most important thing of all is to have fun when printing!

You can take inspiration for your printing work from a number of different sources. It is often a good idea to draw out and paint your design first. This beautiful Egyptian design was first painted on to paper using an opaque watercolour paint called gouache. It was then made into a printing plate in about 1850 and used for printing textiles. It is not known who the artist was, but their design is now in the Design Library in New York, USA.

Natural Wrapping Paper and Gift Tag

YOU WILL NEED
Selection of leaves
Paper • Thin coloured card
Newspaper • Roller
Dye-based ink pad
String • Scissors
Hole punch

You can use many natural objects to print with. Look around the garden for flat stones and pieces of bark or ask for a slice of your favourite fruit or vegetable. This project uses a real leaf.

When choosing your leaf look for a flat, fresh one. Turn it over and feel the back. Leaves that have veins that you can feel are the best for printing. There are so many different trees to choose from – oak, maple, beech and sycamore to name a few.

 Ink up the leaf using a rubber roller and a dye-based ink pad. Roll over the leaf a few times.

 Choose a leaf with an obvious vein pattern.

 Press the leaf firmly on to the paper. Smooth over it with your fingers.

 Repeat the leaf pattern all over the paper. Leave to dry.

5 Cut out a rectangle of thin card and fold it in half to make a gift tag. Use a hole punch to make a hole in the folded edge.

6 Print a leaf on the gift tag. Loop a piece of string through the hole and tie to secure.

FURTHER IDEAS
Try using your leaf design on envelopes, writing paper, cards and invitations.

Sea Monster Game

The inspiration for this fun fishing game comes from the classical sea monsters which feature in the tales of Ancient Greek mythology. You can use textured objects such as bubblewrap and cotton reels to print your own double-headed sea serpents and giant squid. You will need small, round magnets to make this game. These are available from craft shops.

I have used seven sea monsters for this game, but you can make any odd number. For details of how to play the game, turn to page 27.

YOU WILL NEED

Textured objects, e.g. bubblewrap, cotton reels, scouring pads, sponges
Thin card • Scrap paper • Newspaper
Tracing paper • Carbon paper
Masking tape • Water-based paint
Sponge roller • Paintbrush
7 paperclips • 2 magnets
2 pencils • Scissors
String

1 Transfer a mythical sea monster shape on to a piece of thin card (see pages 26–27). Cut it out. Repeat until you have seven sea monsters in total.

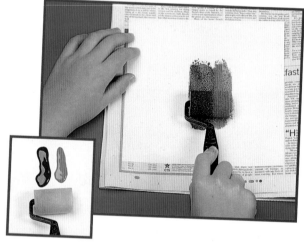

2 Place two stripes of different coloured paint on a piece of scrap paper. Run a sponge roller over both colours at once.

3 Choose a textured object such as bubblewrap, then use the roller to apply paint to one side of it. Turn the bubblewrap over then press it down on to the cut-out sea monster. Peel off to reveal the printed pattern. Leave to dry.

Continue, using different objects and colours, until all the sea monsters are decorated. Paint in the eyes then leave to dry. Repeat steps 2–4 on the back of all the sea monsters.

5 Attach a paperclip to the mouth of each sea monster.

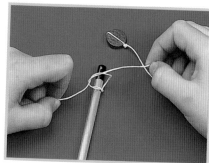

Tie a small magnet on to a piece of string. Tie the other end of the string on to a pencil. You are now ready to play the game.

FURTHER IDEAS
Tie your sea monsters to a coat hanger to create a colourful mobile.

Chinese Pencil Pot

If you are always losing your pencils and pens then this is the project for you. The pot is decorated with Chinese-style printed paper and gold trim is used to add the finishing touch.

A paint paste is spread thickly all over the paper then the design is created by scraping some of the paste away with a cardboard comb so that the paper shows through underneath. For best results use white paper and a darker coloured paint.

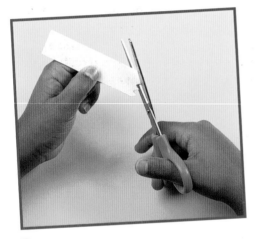

1 Use scissors to cut little V-shaped notches at one end of a small rectangle of cardboard to make a comb.

2 Mix up one cup of wallpaper paste with two teaspoons of paint and one teaspoon of washing-up liquid. Brush the paste mixture thickly on to your paper using a paintbrush.

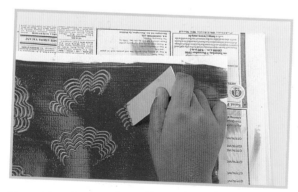

3 Use the cardboard comb to drag a pattern into the paste. Wipe the comb on some newspaper when it becomes clogged with paint.

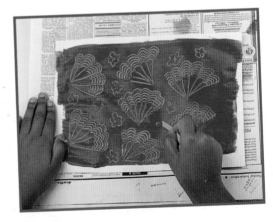

4 Use a small strip of cardboard to add details. Work quickly before the paste dries. When finished, leave to dry.

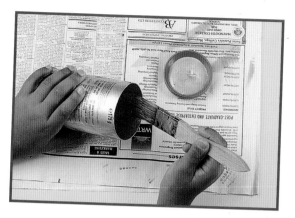

5 Cut the top off a length of tubing. Paint the inside to match your trim.

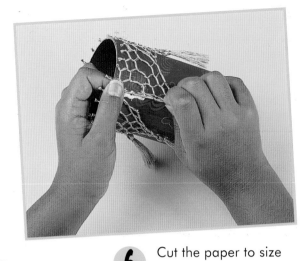

6 Cut the paper to size and glue around the side of the tubing to cover it. Finish by gluing a length of trim around the top.

FURTHER IDEAS

You can use this technique to cover a book or a small box.

Gecko T-shirt

The idea for this design comes from the paintings the Native American Indians used to decorate their tepees. I have chosen a gecko lizard for this T-shirt, but they painted many other designs. Some were used to encourage good spirits and fortunes. The paints they used were made from plants and soil, so the colours were natural and earthy.

This type of printing is called mono printing. Mono means 'one', and with this method of printing you can only make one print. This technique is ideal for transferring a colourful design on to fabric.

 Transfer the gecko design shown on page 27 on to paper (see page 26). Place a sheet of acetate over the design and tape it in place.

2 Paint over one section of the design using one colour of fabric paint.

3 Turn the acetate face down on to the front of your T-shirt. Rub over the back of the acetate with your hand.

4 Carefully peel off the acetate. Touch up the colour with a paintbrush if necessary.

FURTHER IDEAS
Use glow-in-the-dark paint to create a unique T-shirt.

5 Repeat steps 1–4 with other colours to complete the design. Remember to line up the image carefully each time. When complete, leave the paint to dry thoroughly for twenty-four hours.

6 Turn the T-shirt inside out and place a piece of paper inside it. Iron over the design on the reverse side of the T-shirt. Ironing will fix the paints so that the colours do not come out when the T-shirt is washed.

> **(!)** Make sure an adult helps you to iron the T-shirt.

Aztec Birthday Card

Bright, earthy colours and an Aztec sun design are used to create the Mexican theme for this original, hand-printed birthday card.

A piece of smooth, firm polystyrene (like that used for fast-food packaging) is used to create a printing block. This type of block can be used over and over again, so you can print lots of cards using the same design.

1 Cut out a small square of polystyrene.

2 Transfer the sun design shown on page 27 on to the polystyrene (see page 26). Use a blunt pencil to score over the design.

3 Press the front of the polystyrene square on to a rainbow ink pad.

4 Press the polystyrene printing block into the corner of a piece of folded coloured card. Repeat in each corner.

5 Print the image on to a different coloured card, and then cut it out.

6 Glue the design into the centre of the folded card.

FURTHER IDEAS
You can decorate an envelope to match your card.

Egyptian Dominoes

The Ancient Egyptians used pictures called hieroglyphics to tell stories. Hieroglyphic designs are used in this project to create picture dominoes as a variation on the traditional dominoes game. For details about how to play the game, turn to page 28.

You can create wonderfully detailed printing blocks by carving a design into an eraser using a lino cutter. An eraser is soft enough to cut into easily and it transfers the paint well when you start printing.

YOU WILL NEED

6 erasers • Lino cutter
Water-based paint • Paintbrush
Sponge • Coloured card
Newspaper • Tracing paper
Carbon paper
Pencil • Marker pen
Scissors • Ruler

1 Transfer the six designs shown on page 28 on to six erasers (see page 26). Go over the outlines using a marker pen.

2 Use a lino cutter to carve out the areas around and within the designs. Cut with the blade pointing away, not towards you.

A lino cutter is sharp. Make sure you get an adult to help you when you use it.

3 Use a ruler and pencil to mark out twenty-one identical rectangles on coloured card large enough to print two images on. Cut them out using scissors.

4 Use a sponge to apply paint to one of the designs on one of the erasers.

Press the eraser on to one end of one of the card rectangles. Repeat step 4 and continue printing. Make sure that each domino is different and that you have used each stamp six times.

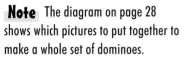 **Note** The diagram on page 28 shows which pictures to put together to make a whole set of dominoes.

6 Add detailing to each of the designs using coloured paint and a paintbrush.

FURTHER IDEAS

Print one image on each piece of card. Make sure you have at least four of each design. Use these to play 'snap' with.

Modern Art Socks

You can get many great design ideas from looking at the work of modern artists. Try to recreate the colours and the patterns they have used. The designs in this project are inspired by the work of the French artist, Matisse.

Ordinary potatoes are used to print bold, lively images on to plain socks. Your potatoes will need to be quite fresh, so that they are still hard. Remember that the size of your design will be limited by the size of your potato.

Place the card template inside the sock.

1 Place one of your socks on a piece of thin card, then draw around it with a pencil. Cut out the shape.

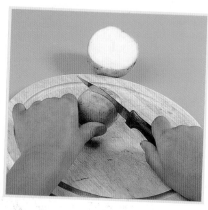

Vegetable knives are very sharp. Get an adult to help when you cut the potatoes.

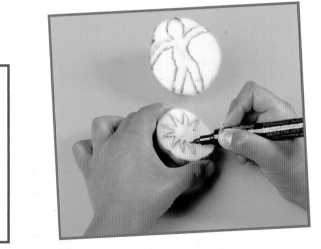

3 Place two potatoes on a chopping board. Cut them in half using a vegetable knife.

4 Use a marker pen to copy the designs shown on page 29 on to the potatoes.

Get an adult to help you cut out the designs.

5 Use a vegetable knife to cut down around the edge of the design, then across from the side of the potato.

6 Paint over the raised designs with fabric paint, then print them on to your sock. Repeat all the steps to decorate the other sock. Iron to fix the colours (see page 13).

FURTHER IDEAS
You can decorate lots of items using this technique — baseball hats, canvas shoes or T-shirts, for example.

Mosaic Chalk Board

Mosaic designs are normally made by cutting glass or coloured tiles into small pieces then cementing them on to a wall or floor to create a picture or pattern. The Ancient Greeks and Romans are famous for mosaics.

In this project, a piece of high-density foam is cut into small squares and stuck to a wooden block. The block is then used to print instant mosaic designs. You could use thick cardboard instead of wood, but this means that you cannot wash and re-use the block. Before you begin, measure your chalk board and decide what size the designs need to be before you trace them from page 29.

YOU WILL NEED
Chalk board
High-density foam
Square and rectangular wood off-cuts
or thick cardboard
Water-based paints • Paintbrush
Newspaper • Carbon paper
Tracing paper • Masking tape
Pencil • Scissors
PVA glue

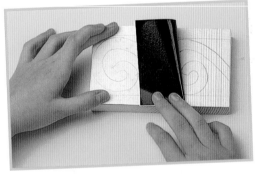

1 Transfer the designs shown on page 31 on to square and rectangular pieces of wood (see page 26).

2 Use scissors to cut a piece of high-density foam into small squares. Cut some of these squares into smaller, odd-shaped pieces.

3 Glue the square foam pieces on to each piece of wood, following the lines of the designs. Fill in the gaps with the small odd-shaped pieces of foam.

4 Paint over the raised foam images on both the square and rectangular printing blocks. Change colours where appropriate.

Press the square stamp on to one of the corners of the chalk board. Carefully lift the block off, apply more paint, then repeat at each corner.

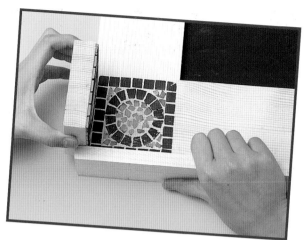

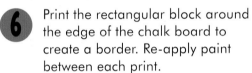 Print the rectangular block around the edge of the chalk board to create a border. Re-apply paint between each print.

FURTHER IDEAS

You can use this technique to decorate the rim of an indoor plant pot.

Asian Cushion

This sumptuous cushion is printed with a design inspired by traditional Asian arts. The design is known as paisley and is often used to decorate the elaborate saris worn by Asian women. In India and surrounding countries, very bright colours are popular for clothes and decorations.

The printing block for this project is made out of string glued to a piece of thin card. For best results choose string that is smooth, thick and quite stiff, as this will hold its shape well.

YOU WILL NEED

Plain cushion
String • Thin card • Paper
Carbon paper • Tracing paper
Masking tape • Pencil • Scissors
Fabric paint • Sponge
Tea towel or piece of cloth
Iron and ironing board
PVA glue

 Transfer the paisley design shown on page 29 on to a piece of thin card. Cut it out, leaving a small border around the edge.

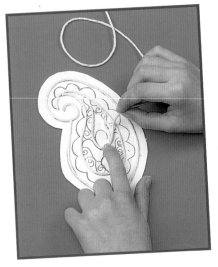

Glue string on to the card, following the line of the design.

 Apply fabric paint on to the string using a sponge.

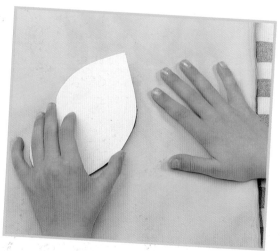

4

Place the cushion on a smooth and soft surface such as a folded tea towel. This will make it easier to print the design. Press the painted side of the string design on to the plain cushion.

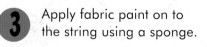

5 Repeat steps 3–4 to cover the cushion, applying more paint to the string each time you make a print. Iron to fix the design (see page 13). (!)

6 Place the cushion pad back inside the cover.

FURTHER IDEAS
You can use this technique to decorate a plain shoebag.

Primitive Clay Picture

The first recorded forms of art were the paintings on cave walls which were made by early settlers. The paintings usually showed images of men and animals and were painted in muted shades of red and brown. Like the Native Indians, early settlers used soil and clay to create a type of paint.

You can create your own cave paintings by printing with pipe cleaners into air-drying clay. The clay is soft, so you can push the pipe cleaner shapes into the clay to leave an impression. When the clay has dried, it can be painted with earthy colours.

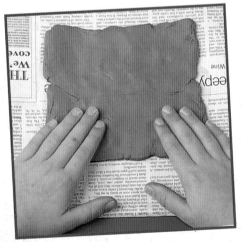

1 Photocopy and enlarge the pattern shown on page 29 (see page 26). Bend pipe cleaners to follow the lines of the designs.

2 Work small sections at a time, cutting the pipe cleaners as you go. Join the pieces together by twisting them.

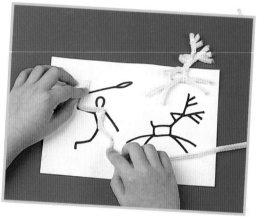

3 Press a piece of clay with your fingers to flatten it into a square shape.

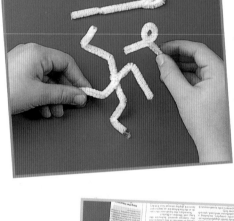

4 Press the pipe cleaner designs into the clay to leave an impression. Remove them carefully then leave the clay to dry for twenty-four hours.

5 Sponge earthy-coloured paints randomly over the clay to create the effect of stone.

6 Use a paintbrush to paint around the shape of the designs so that they stand out.

FURTHER IDEAS
You can use this technique to make an unusual paperweight.

Patterns

You can trace the patterns on these pages straight from the book (follow steps 1–4). Alternatively, you can make them larger or smaller on a photocopier if you wish, and then follow steps 2–4.

Get an adult to help you photocopy the patterns.

Transferring a pattern on to another surface

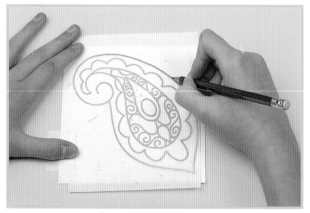

1 Place a piece of tracing paper over the pattern and then tape it down with small pieces of masking tape. Trace around the outline using a soft pencil.

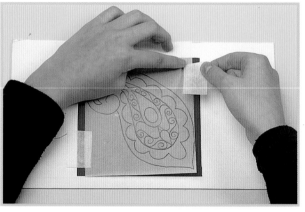

2 Place carbon paper on the surface you want to transfer the design on to. Place the tracing over the top and tape it in place.

3 Trace over the outline with a pencil.

4 Remove the tracing paper and carbon paper to reveal the transferred image.

Patterns for the Sea Monster Game
featured on pages 8–9.

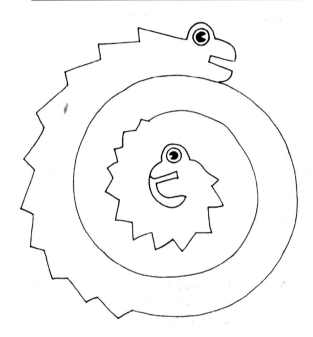

Rules for the Sea Monster Game

To play the game, pile up all the monsters, then use your pencil fishing rod to try and catch one. If you manage to lift it from the pile without entangling the others then you get to keep the monster. If not, put it back and let the next person have a turn. The winner is the person who has got the most monsters when the pile has gone.

Pattern for the Gecko T-shirt
featured on pages 12–13.

Pattern for the Aztec Birthday
Card featured on pages 14–15.

| 1 | 1 | 1 | 2 | 1 | 3 | 1 | 4 | 1 | 5 | 1 | 6 |

| 2 | 2 | 2 | 3 | 2 | 4 | 2 | 5 | 2 | 6 |

| 3 | 3 | 3 | 4 | 3 | 5 | 3 | 6 |

| 4 | 4 | 4 | 5 | 4 | 6 |

| 5 | 5 | 5 | 6 |

| 6 | 6 |

The patterns shown below are for the Egyptian Dominoes featured on pages 16–17. They have all been given a number. Print your dominoes in the combinations shown here.

1

2

3

4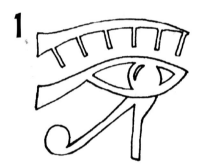

5

6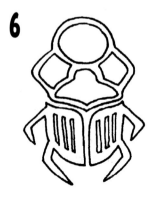

Rules for Dominoes

To play the game, deal each player seven dominoes face down. Leave the rest in a pile face down. Player 1 places a domino on the table; player 2 looks through their dominoes for a matching picture, and places that domino next to the first so that the pictures touch. Play continues in this way until a player cannot put a domino down. This player must pick up one of the spare dominoes and continue play. The winner is the first person to put down all of their dominoes. You can match two pictures at either end of the domino, and doubles can be played sideways.

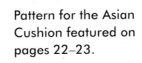

Pattern for the Asian
Cushion featured on
pages 22–23.

Patterns for the Modern Art Socks
featured on pages 18–19. These
cannot be transferred on to a potato
using the technique shown on page
26, so you will need to copy them
carefully yourself. Adjust the sizes
according to the sizes of your potatoes.

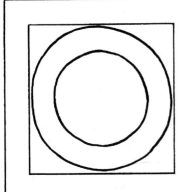

Patterns for the Mosaic Chalk
Board featured on pages 20–21.

Patterns for the Primitive Clay
Picture featured on pages 24–25.

Creative Lettering
by Judy Balchin

Imagine a world with no letters – no books, signs or labels, no way to leave a message for your parents or to write to friends. Well, that is how it was a long time ago. There were no letters; they actually had to be invented.

Many years ago the American Indians used pictures called pictograms as a memory guide to remind them of events and songs when telling stories. As time went on and more complicated information needed to be exchanged or remembered, symbols were created to represent ideas or things. We can still see this today in the Chinese alphabet. Every idea or thing has its own symbol and believe it or not, a Chinese scholar must know over fifteen thousand symbols to write his books. The ancient Egyptians used another complicated system called hieroglyphics. We all know our ABC, but did you know that the letter A was once a hieroglyphic symbol of an eagle and B was a crane?

Over time, alphabets had to change and become simpler. The first simple alphabet was invented in Assyria in the fourteenth century BC. It was called cuneiform and was made up of lines and wedge shapes. It had thirty letters and was used by merchants to record their business dealings. The twenty-six letters we use today are derived from the Greek alphabet. In fact the word 'alphabet' is made from the first two letters of the Greek alphabet, alpha and beta.

We are surrounded by letters. Advertisers are extremely competitive and creative with their lettering styles as they entice you to buy their product. Perhaps you could try having a 'letter awareness' day. Get up in the morning, brush your teeth and look at the lettering on your toothpaste tube. Read the cereal packet over breakfast and see what letters are used. Look at book covers at school and while you eat your lunch, study the food wrappers. Television too offers us a variety of letter styles. It is amazing just how creative you can be with letters.

Now that you know the wonderful history of the alphabet and just how important lettering is to our everyday lives, we can have some fun. By the time you have worked your way through this section you will be able to tell the difference between 'serif' and 'sans serif' letters. You will notice 'drop shadows' on letters and begin to understand how important colour is. With a few pens and some paper you will be able to create your own letters and make cards, invitations, writing paper, bookmarks, posters and much more. I hope that this section inspires you to continue with this fascinating hobby.

Opposite *This colourful page from a Book of Hours was written and illustrated in Italy in about 1500 AD. The large letter D has been decorated with leaves and a picture of King David at prayer. Books of Hours contained pictures and short prayers – each suitable for a particular hour of the day. They became so popular that artists had to employ many assistants to help them produce enough books.*

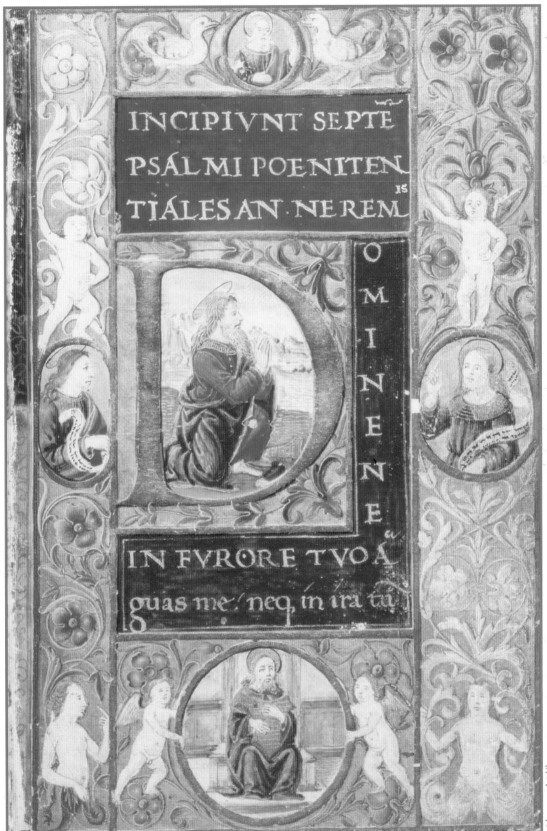

INCIPIVNT SEPTE
PSALMI POENITEN
TIALES AN NEREM
DOMINENE
IN FVRORE TVO A
guas me: neq, in ira tu

Techniques

Take time to read through this techniques section before you start the projects. The alphabets and patterns that you will need are on pages 50–55. You can transfer them on to your paper with transfer paper.

Ask an adult to help you enlarge the letters and patterns on a photocopier.

Transferring letters and patterns

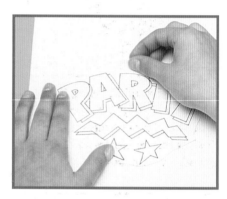

 1 Enlarge the pattern on a photocopier and cut it out. Lay it on a sheet of paper and tape the top with a piece of masking tape.

2 Slip the transfer paper face-down under the pattern and tape it at the bottom to keep it in place.

 3 Trace around the outline of the pattern with a pencil to transfer the design on to the paper.

 4 Remove the transfer paper, then go over the outline with a black pen. Leave to dry for five minutes.

 5 Rub out any lines or smudges with an eraser and fill in the design with coloured pens.

Note Remember to put the tops back on your pens.

Copying letters

You will be asked to copy letters from the alphabets at the back of the book. Planning your lettering is important. Always work in pencil before going over the letters with a pen.

1 Lightly draw in the guidelines for the lettering. A guideline is the line on which your letters sit. It may be straight, curved or wavy.

2 Pencil in the letters using the alphabet as a guide (see page 50). This dot serif alphabet is the easiest one to start with as it is based on neat writing.

Note Cut a star shape around the design, or choose your own shape.

3 Go over the pencilled letters with a coloured pen, adding dots to the ends and joints of the letters. When the pen has dried, remove any visible pencil lines with an eraser.

Rocket Birthday Card

Make your own dazzling range of cards using coloured pens and paper. The 'dot serif' alphabet used here is the easiest alphabet to create. All you have to do is print your message clearly, then add dots to the ends and joints of the letters. You can bring a sense of movement into the words by slanting the letters in different ways. A pattern has been provided (see page 31), but you might like to try this project without using the pattern. Practise on scrap paper first.

YOU WILL NEED

White paper
Coloured felt-tipped pens
Metallic card • Black felt-tipped pen
Metallic marker pen
Transfer paper • Masking tape
Pencil • Eraser • Scissors
PVA glue

1 Transfer the pattern from page 55 on to white paper (see page 32).

2 Go over the outlines with a black felt-tipped pen. Leave to dry then rub out all the pencil lines.

3 Run a coloured line around the black lettering.

4 Colour in the rocket, then use a metallic pen to decorate it with two rows of dots. Draw stars between the letters to fill in any spaces.

5 Cut out the design.

6 Fold a sheet of metallic card in half and glue your design in place.

FURTHER IDEAS
You can create lots of cards for other occasions. Decorate them with colourful shapes and images.

Balloon Party Invitation

Send a special party invitation to your friends. A 'sans serif' alphabet with a 'drop shadow' is used for the lettering. Serifs are the lines that extend across the ends of the letters and 'Sans serif' means without serifs. Compare the alphabets on pages 52 and 53 to see the difference between 'serif' and 'sans serif' letters. A 'drop shadow' is a thick line which is usually drawn down one side and along the bottom of a letter, which makes it really stand out. This type of lettering is often used on food and sweet wrappers as it is bold and eye-catching.

YOU WILL NEED
Coloured card
Coloured felt-tipped pens
Black felt-tipped pen
Curling ribbon • Transfer paper
Masking tape • Pencil
Scissors • Eraser

1 Transfer the basic pattern from page 31 on to coloured card (see page 32). Go over the outline of the letters and designs with a black felt-tipped pen. Fill in the drop shadow.

2 Draw two curved lines on the top half of the balloon. Lightly pencil in 'you are invited to a' using the alphabet on page 50 as a guide.

3 Outline the lettering with a brightly coloured pen. Leave to dry for a few minutes, then rub out any visible pencil lines.

36

Fill in the word 'party' and the zig-zag shape underneath with the same colour. Fill in the stars using a different colour, then add some curly lines.

5 Cut out the invitation. Tie a piece of paper ribbon around the knot of the balloon.

6 Lightly pencil in some guidelines on the back of the invitation, then write down your message.

FURTHER IDEAS
Write your name in the balloon and fill in the letters with lots of different colours.

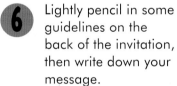

Alien Door Plaque

A design can look fun if you combine an illustration with the lettering and then decorate each letter with different colours and patterns. The door plaque uses the 'line serif' alphabet on page 29, where lines are drawn across the ends of the letters, so that they extend slightly beyond the letter. Can you spot 'serif' letters in your books?

YOU WILL NEED
White card
Black felt-tipped pen
Coloured felt-tipped pens
Transfer paper • Masking tape
Pencil • Eraser
Scissors

1 Transfer the pattern shown on page 55 on to white card (see page 32), then go over the outline with a black felt-tipped pen. Leave to dry.

2 Fill in each of the letters with a different design. Use lots of colours.

3 Use the dot serif alphabet on page 50 to pencil in 'my room' underneath and then outline with a coloured pen. Leave to dry and rub out all the pencil lines.

4 Colour in the alien.

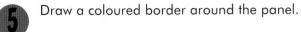

5 Draw a coloured border around the panel.

6 Cut out the plaque, leaving a small border around the edge.

FURTHER IDEAS

Use another alphabet and different colours to personalise a journal, school book or notebook.

Ask an adult to help you attach the plaque to your door. You can use low-tack masking tape or removable adhesive.

Illuminated Bookmark

The inspiration for this project is taken from beautifully illuminated old manuscripts. These were created by monks using quill pens and paints, and the first capital letter on a page was always decorated with gold leaf and bright colours. Water-based paint and a metallic marker pen are used to create an illuminated bookmark. Use a dark colour for your own initial so that the metallic pen work really stands out.

YOU WILL NEED

Dark coloured card
Light coloured paper
Metallic marker pen
Water-based paint • Small paintbrush
Transfer paper • Masking Tape
Pencil • Eraser • Ruler
Scissors • PVA glue
Hole punch • Ribbon

1 Transfer a letter from the alphabet on page 50 on to light coloured paper (see page 32). Paint it using a dark colour. Leave to dry.

2 Use the alphabet pattern as a guide. Outline the letter and swirls with a metallic marker pen. Draw the inner lines. Leave to dry.

3 With a ruler and pencil, draw a square around the letter. Cut around the square leaving a small border, then tear the edges following the lines.

 4

Draw a rectangle on dark card and tear the edges. Colour the edges of the square and the rectangle with a metallic marker pen.

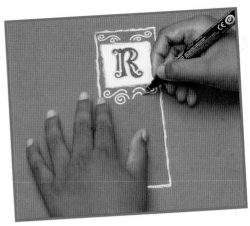

 5

Punch a hole at the top of the rectangle with a hole punch and glue the letter below it. Add swirls around the square with the metallic pen, then transfer the pattern shown on page 55 on to the area below the letter (see page 32).

6

Thread the bookmark with matching ribbon. Fold the ribbon in half, push the loop through the hole and pull the ends through the loop.

FURTHER IDEAS

By changing the initial and the colours you can make bookmarks for all your friends.

Personalised Paper

Creating your own personalised writing paper will give your letters a distinctive look. The letters are drawn in boxes which are cut out, arranged on a sheet of paper, then glued into place. The design can be photocopied many times and each copy can then be decorated with colours and motifs of your choice.

YOU WILL NEED

White paper
Black felt-tipped pen
Coloured felt-tipped pens
Ruler • Pencil
Scissors • PVA glue

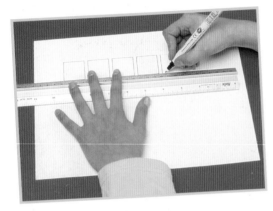

1 Count the letters in your first name. Draw the same number of 3cm (1¼in) squares on a piece of paper and outline them with a black felt-tipped pen.

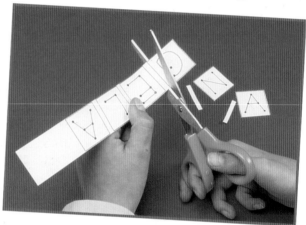

2 Choose an alphabet from the back of the book (see pages 50–54). Use a pencil to copy each letter of your name on to a square. Go over the outline of the letters with a black felt-tipped pen. Leave to dry, rub out any visible pencil lines, then cut out the squares.

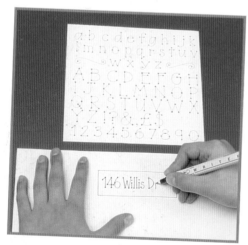

3 Draw a rectangle 3cm x 9cm (1¼in x 3¾in) and outline it in black. Write your address within it and then cut out the rectangle.

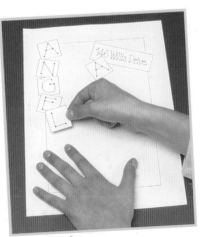

4 Use a ruler to draw a border line 3 cm (1¼in) from the edges of a sheet of white paper. Glue the squares down the left-hand edge of the border, then glue the rectangle in the bottom right-hand corner.

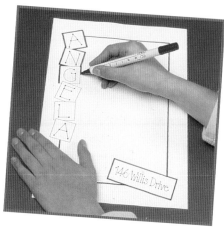

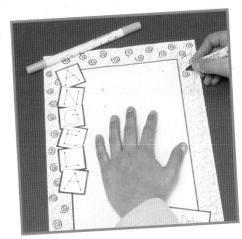

 6 Cover the outer border with a swirling pattern using a pale colour, then decorate it with darker spirals.

 5 Photocopy your letterhead as many times as you wish. Edge the border, the address panel and each square with a coloured pen.

> **(!)** Ask an adult to help you photocopy the letterhead.

FURTHER IDEAS

Choose a different alphabet and photocopy your design on to coloured paper. Decorate the border with squares, triangles or circles.

Snow White Poster

Large letters and bright colours are needed for a title when you are making a poster.

This makes it more eye-catching.

It is easier to cut the letters out of paper and to arrange them on a card base along with an information panel. When you are satisfied with the design, glue all the letters down.

YOU WILL NEED

Coloured and white paper
Sparkly card
Coloured card
Tracing paper • Pencil
Coloured felt-tipped pens
Scissors • PVA glue

(!) Ask an adult to help you enlarge the letters on a photocopier.

1 Trace the letters for the title using the alphabet on page 54. Enlarge the letters on a photocopier so that the longest word fits comfortably across a sheet of paper. Cut the letters out.

2 Lay the letters on the sparkly card and draw around them.

3 Cut the letters out and arrange them across the top of the coloured card. Glue them in position. Cut and glue a rectangle of sparkly card to fit within the bottom half of the card.

Cut out a piece of white paper slightly smaller than the rectangle of sparkly card. Using the letters on page 50 as a guide, pencil your message on to the white rectangle. Go over the words with coloured pens.

6

Cut out stars from coloured paper and glue them around the edge of your poster.

5 Glue the panel on to the sparkly card.

FURTHER IDEAS

Make more posters to broadcast special messages or school news. Illustrate them with different shapes and patterns.

Hobby Box

The style and decoration of lettering tells us quite a lot. This container needs a bold, brightly coloured label which shouts 'paints'. The letters have a drop shadow and are overlapped slightly to give them a three dimensional look. The colours of the box and label complement each other, which creates a bright, stylish look.

YOU WILL NEED

Round cardboard box 16cm diameter x 10cm high (6¼in x 4in)
White paper • Pencil
Black felt-tipped pen
Coloured felt-tipped pens • Scissors
Acrylic paints
Small and large paintbrushes
PVA glue

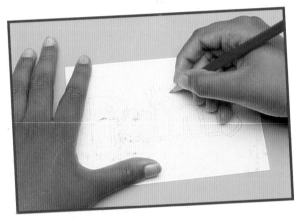

1 Draw the guidelines on white paper with a pencil. Copy the word 'Paints' using the alphabet on page 52 as a guide. Replace the dot over the 'i' with a splash shape, then add a drop shadow to the splash.

2 Use a black felt-tipped pen to go over the outlines of the letters, then fill in the drop shadow. Run wavy lines along the top of the letters to look like dripping paint.

3 Fill in the letters with a bright colour, then fill in the splash and drips with different colours.

4 Cut around the letters, leaving a 0.5cm (¼in) border of white paper.

46

5 Use acrylic paints and a large paintbrush to paint the box and lid with bright colours. Draw splash shapes over the lid with a black felt-tipped pen. Leave to dry, then paint them in with bright colours using a small paintbrush.

6 Glue the finished label to the front of the box.

FURTHER IDEAS

Make a jewellery box using pastel colours and sparkly letters, or a treasure box using metallic colours.

School Project Folder

By now you will be getting more confident with your lettering. This project is great fun and you can really be creative! Each letter is transformed into an illustration. The first letter is 'P' – and P is for pencil, so you could draw a pencil in the shape of the letter P. The next letter is 'R' and R is for ribbon. Try to think of different things for each letter in the word 'Project'.

YOU WILL NEED
Coloured folder
Pencil • Ruler
White paper
Black felt-tipped pen
Coloured felt-tipped pens
PVA glue

1 Spend a little time planning what you want the letters to be. Write them down on a piece of paper and alongside each one make a list of things beginning with that letter. Try drawing a few of them to see how they will look.

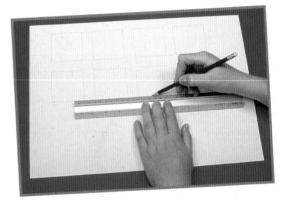

2 Use a pencil and ruler to draw seven 6cm (2¼in) squares on a piece of white paper. Leave a gap of about 3cm (1¼in) between the squares.

3 Use a pencil and draw one illustrated letter on each square.

4 Go over the outlines of each letter with a black felt-tipped pen, then fill them in with different colours.

5 Cut around each box, leaving a small border. Now tear the edges of the squares following the lines.

6 Place the torn squares on a scrap piece of paper. Add a coloured border around the edges of each square.

7 Arrange the squares on your folder, then glue them into place.

FURTHER IDEAS

Create an alphabet using a different animal for each letter, or decorate your folder with fantasy figures.

Alphabets

These alphabets can be copied or traced on to tracing paper, then transferred on to your writing surface with transfer paper. They can also be enlarged on a photocopier if you are making a poster.

Dot serif

Illuminated

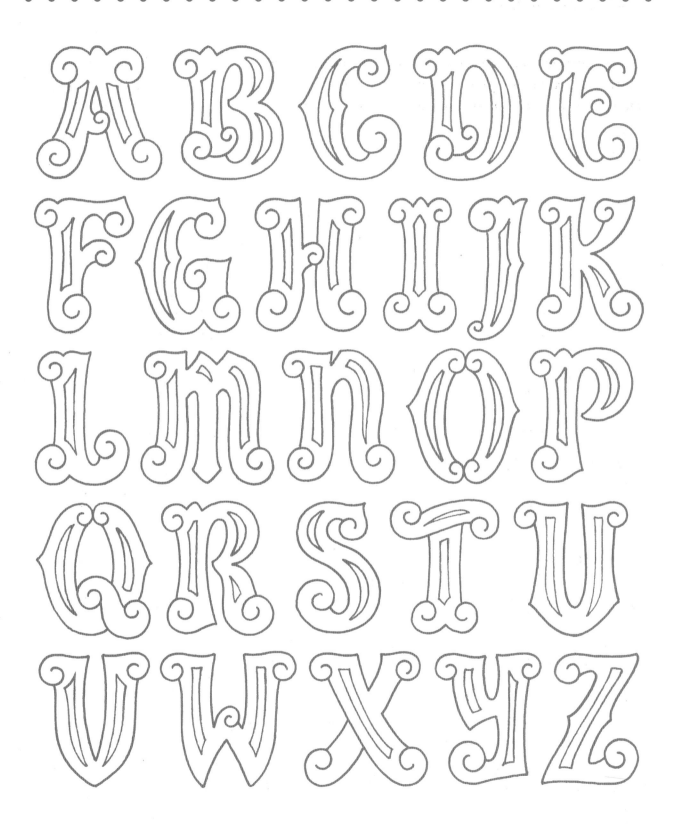

Block sans serif with drop shadow

abcdefghij
klmnopqrs
tuvwxyz
ABCDEFG
HIJKLMN
OPQRSTU
VWXYZ!?&,£$
1234567890

Line serif

abcdefghij
klmnopqrs
tuvwxyz
ABCDEFG
HIJKLMN
OPQRSTUV
WXYZ!?&£$
1234567890

Rounded sans serif

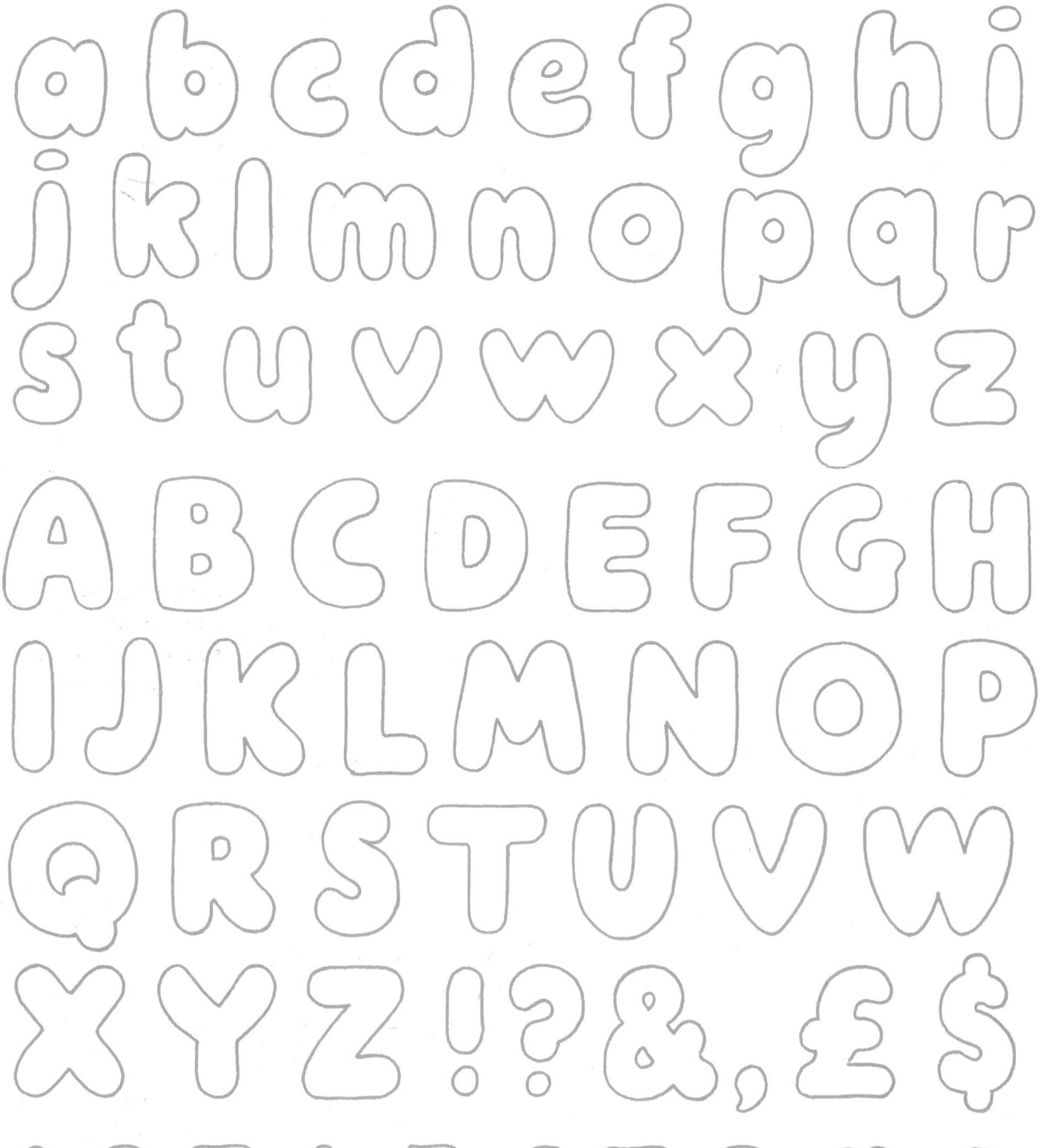

a b c d e f g h i
j k l m n o p q r
s t u v w x y z
A B C D E F G H
I J K L M N O P
Q R S T U V W
X Y Z ! ? & , £ $
1 2 3 4 5 6 7 8 9 0

Patterns

*Pattern for the Alien
Door Plaque featured
on pages 38–39.*

*Pattern for the Illuminated
Bookmark featured
on pages 40–41.*

*Pattern for
the Balloon
Party Invitation
featured on
pages 36–37.*

*Pattern for the Rocket Birthday
Card featured on pages 34–35.*

Mosaics

by Michelle Powell

Traditional mosaics are beautiful works of art. They are created with many small pieces of clay, glass, stone and other hard materials, which are set closely together on a firm surface to create a decorative design or picture.

The earliest mosaics date back to 3000 BC when they were usually created as a type of floor decoration made of small coloured pebbles. Later, glass, marble and clay were coloured then cut into small cubes or tiles. These were used to decorate the floors, walls and ceilings inside important buildings. A thick layer of plaster would be applied to the wall, then a picture or design was painted on to the surface while it was still wet. Before the plaster dried, matching coloured cubes or tiles were pushed into the surface to create the mosaic.

Large mosaics took a long time to make and were expensive, so they were very precious and a sign of great wealth. They were mostly used to decorate the inside of churches and religious buildings. Early Christian mosaics show figures and animals with decorative borders. In Islam, temples were decorated with beautiful designs of leaves and palm trees with a vibrant gold background. The Greeks often decorated their floors with dark and light pebble mosaics.

The ancient Egyptians made mosaic jewellery for their kings by setting tiny pieces of turquoise, precious stones and enamel into gold. On page 66 you will see how you can create a similar type of jewellery using pasta painted gold and turquoise. Gold and turquoise were also used to decorate statues and pottery items made by the ancient craft workers of Latin America. The Greeks and Romans made huge mosaics from handmade coloured clay tiles and our coaster project on page 70 shows you how to make your own clay mosaic tiles.

Some early mosaics can still be seen today, as they have not worn away over time. Now, small coloured glass squares and highly glazed clay tiles are especially made, and although they take a long time to create and are very expensive, mosaics are still being made by skilled crafts people.

Opposite The best-known mosaics were made by Roman and Byzantine craft workers. The mosaic pictured on the right was designed to decorate the church of S. Vitale in Ravenna, Italy, in about 530 AD. It shows soldiers at the court of the Byzantine emperor Justinian. Large mosaics were probably designed by companies of artists, and the pieces, the tessarae, were cut before being taken to a building to be stuck in place.

Insect Greetings Card

It is very easy to make attractive mosaic greetings cards for your family and friends using your own drawings or paintings. Make sure you paint or draw them on thick card using brightly coloured, bold designs. Strong images and patterns work best, as fine detail will be lost when the picture is cut into mosaic pieces. Draw a grid on to the front of the picture or photograph (see step 4) and cut along the lines to create your mosaic pieces.

YOU WILL NEED
Thin card
Medium weight card
Carbon paper • Tracing paper
Masking tape • Pencil
Scissors • Ruler
Water-based paints or coloured pens
Paintbrush • Glue stick
Cocktail stick

 Fold a piece of thin card in half and place it to one side.

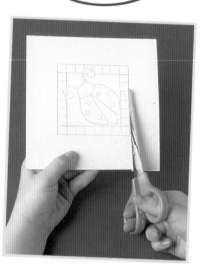

 Transfer the insect pattern shown on page 79 on to a piece of medium weight card. Cut around the edge.

 Use coloured paints or pens to fill in the design.

4 Use a pencil and ruler to join up the lines on the border – to form a grid on the front of the design.

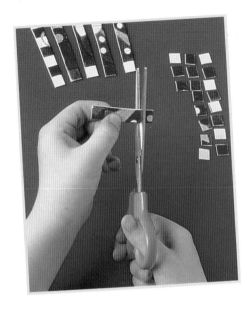

5

Cut along each line using scissors. Carefully lay the pieces down in order as they are cut out.

6 Carefully glue the pieces in the right order on to the front of the folded card. Leave a 2mm ($^1/_{12}$in) gap between each piece, using a cocktail stick as a guide.

FURTHER IDEAS
Use a colour photocopy of a favourite photograph instead of drawing your own picture.

African Mask

Masks were worn in African tribal war dances to make the wearer look more ferocious. The dancers would also use body adornments and sometimes special clothing, which added to the drama and atmosphere of the dance. You can make your own African mosaic mask using small squares and triangles of thin coloured high-density foam, felt or thin card. These soft materials are excellent for masks as they are more comfortable than some of the harder materials that are available.

YOU WILL NEED
Coloured high-density foam
Carbon paper • Tracing paper
Masking tape • Pencil
Scissors • Felt tipped pen
PVA glue • Hole punch
Shearing elastic

1 Transfer the mask pattern shown on page 79 on to a piece of high-density foam. Cut around the basic shape. Hold the mask up to your face, then carefully feel around on the front for the position of your eyes. Ask a friend to mark in their position with a felt-tipped pen, then cut out the eye holes using scissors.

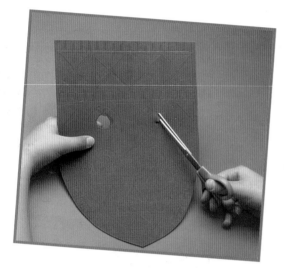

2 Use the pattern as a rough guide. Choosing different colours, cut squares, triangles and wedge shapes from high-density foam.

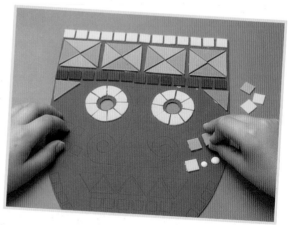

3 Glue the pieces on to the mask using PVA glue.

60

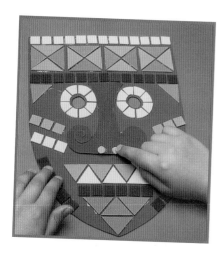

4

Cut out the nose from another piece of high-density foam and glue it into position. Cut out two circles for the nostrils and glue them on to the nose. Leave the glue to dry for half an hour.

5 Use a hole punch to make a hole on either side of the mask, approximately 1cm (½in) in from the edge.

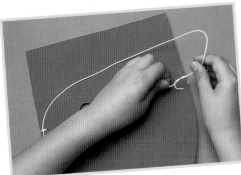

6

Cut a piece of shearing elastic so that it is long enough to fit around your head. Tie each end through the holes in the mask.

FURTHER IDEAS

Choose an animal and make a fun mask, or choose different colours and create your own African mask.

Knight in Armour Picture

In the Middle Ages battling knights wore armour made of metal sheets and chain mail, which protected them from injury. In order to make this knight look more realistic, metal nuts, bolts, screws, washers and chain have been used, along with coloured and silver foils. You do not have to use any of these – just create the knight with whatever you have. Real chain has been used to create the chain mail. You can buy this from most **DIY** and home improvement stores.

YOU WILL NEED
Thick coloured card
Silver and coloured foil
Selection of small nuts, bolts, washers, screws and chain
Carbon paper • Tracing paper
Masking tape • Pencil • Scissors
Water-based paint • Pliers
Small paintbrush
PVA glue

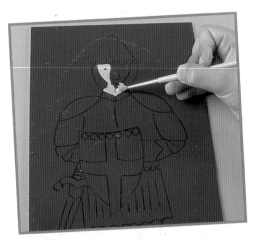

 Transfer the knight in armour and shield patterns shown on page 79 on to a piece of thick card. Paint in the knight's face using a small paintbrush.

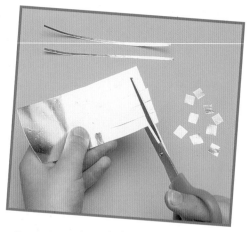

 Cut silver foil into small squares, triangles and wedge shapes for the armour. Cut out two strips long enough for the sword.

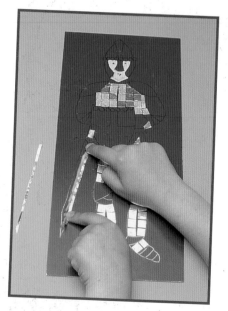

 Glue the foil on to the knight using PVA glue.

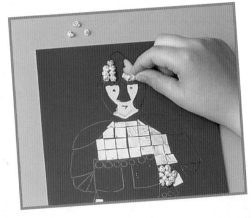

Roll pieces of silver foil into small balls. Use PVA glue to attach them to the cuff on the armour, and the helmet.

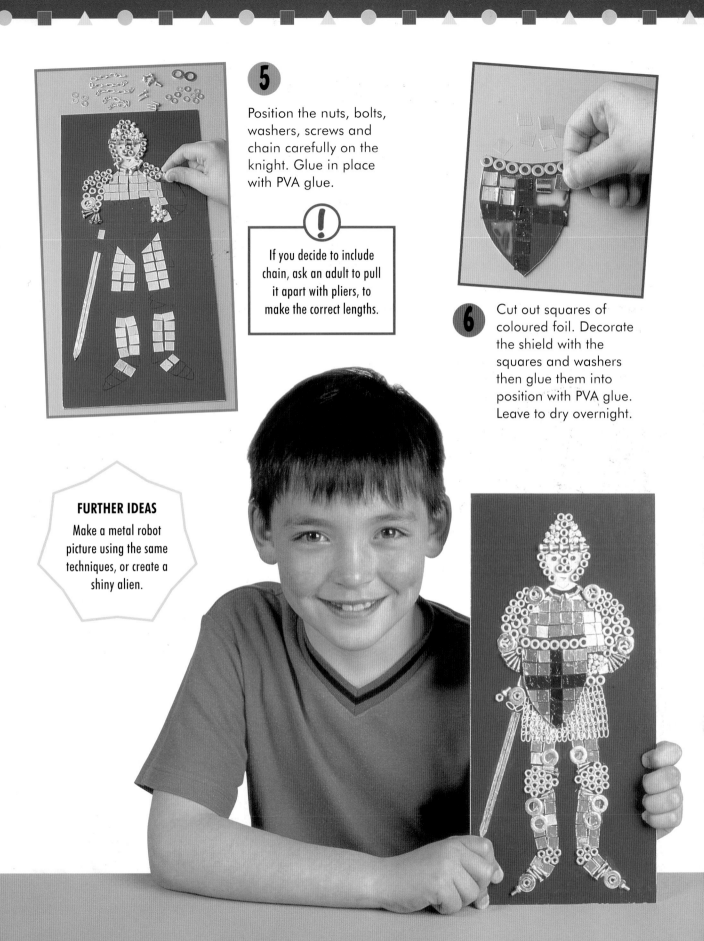

5

Position the nuts, bolts, washers, screws and chain carefully on the knight. Glue in place with PVA glue.

!

If you decide to include chain, ask an adult to pull it apart with pliers, to make the correct lengths.

6

Cut out squares of coloured foil. Decorate the shield with the squares and washers then glue them into position with PVA glue. Leave to dry overnight.

FURTHER IDEAS

Make a metal robot picture using the same techniques, or create a shiny alien.

Indian Elephant Shoebag

In India, elephants are often seen at festivals wearing bright, colourful decorative saddlecloths and elaborate headdresses. Using coloured felt or fabrics, feathers and pretty gold or metallic coloured trims, you can create a fabric Indian elephant mosaic on a plain shoe or toiletries bag. If you do not have one that is suitable, ask an adult to make a simple bag out of a rectangle of fabric. Fold this in half, sew the bottom edges together, then the side edges. Turn the top edge over to the inside to form a hem, then sew along the bottom edge, leaving a gap at the side seam. Thread the cord through the hem and tie a knot at the end.

1 Cut grey felt into small squares and wedge shapes.

2 Transfer the elephant design shown on page 80 on to your shoebag. Stick the grey felt squares and wedge shapes on to the elephant using PVA glue.

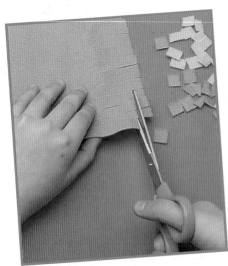

3 Use different colours and cut some more felt into small squares and wedge shapes. Glue them in position.

4

Use PVA glue to attach small feathers to the headdress, and use sequins to decorate the saddlecloth.

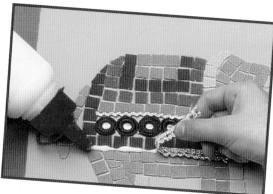

5 Glue metallic coloured trim around the headdress and the base of the saddlecloth.

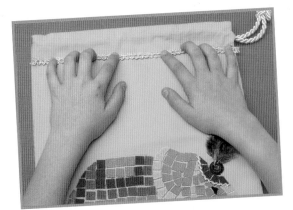

6 Glue metallic coloured trim around the top of the bag to decorate it. Leave to dry overnight.

Note The design on this shoebag is only glued on and therefore the bag should not be washed. If it gets dirty, carefully sponge it clean.

FURTHER IDEAS
Decorate a pencil case, school bag, baseball hat, T-shirt or jacket. Change the colours for different effects.

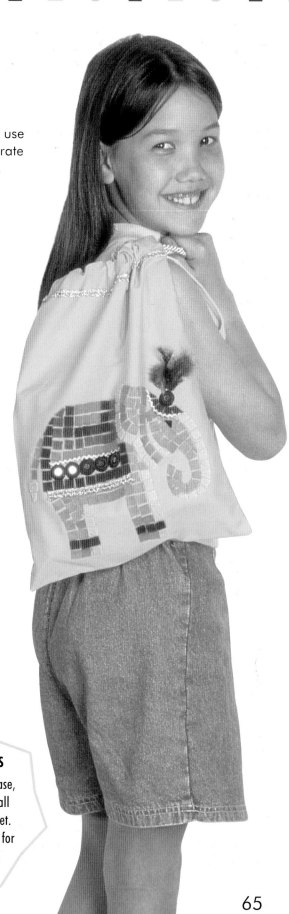

Egyptian Eagle Necklace

Beautiful gold and precious stone jewellery has been found in the tombs of ancient Egyptian pharaohs. You can make your own dazzling Egyptian mosaic jewellery using dried pasta – all sorts of different shapes are available. Look out for small shells and tubes that can be threaded like beads on to shearing elastic. The pasta is painted using coloured and metallic water-based paints in the same colours as the gold and precious stones used in Egyptian jewellery.

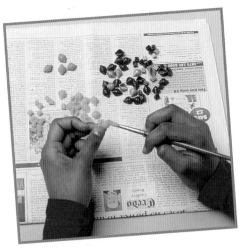

1 Transfer the eagle pattern shown on page 80 on to thick card. Carefully cut it out.

2 Cover your work surface with newspaper. Paint the pasta shells and tubes with metallic and coloured paint. Leave the pieces to dry and wash your hands thoroughly.

Note Do not cook or eat the pasta after it has been painted.

3 Use a hole punch to make three holes at the edge of the eagle's wings.

5

Tie three lengths of shearing elastic through the holes on one side of one wing. Thread pasta tubes on to the elastic.

Note String can be used instead of elastic.

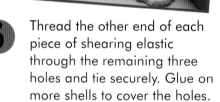

4 Glue the pasta shells and tubes in place using PVA glue.

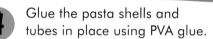

6 Thread the other end of each piece of shearing elastic through the remaining three holes and tie securely. Glue on more shells to cover the holes.

FURTHER IDEAS

Create a scarab beetle bracelet to match your necklace using the same techniques. Or look for other Egyptian designs and make your own jewellery using different colours.

Maths Biscuits

Mosaics can even be created using edible items like the small coloured sweets in this project. Here, candy coated chocolate sweets are attached to plain biscuits using icing. The quantities given make enough icing for four large biscuits. If you want to decorate more, you will need to make more icing. Use everyday kitchen utensils to make the icing and not things that you would normally use for painting, and remember to wash your hands well before you start to decorate the biscuits.

1 Place six heaped dessertspoons of icing sugar into a bowl.

2 Add four teaspoons of lemon juice.

3 Stir the icing and lemon juice together until all the lumps are gone.

Note The icing should be like a stiff paste. If it is too runny, add more icing sugar. If it is too dry, add a drop more lemon juice.

4 Spoon a small quantity of icing over a biscuit and use the back of a teaspoon to spread it out.

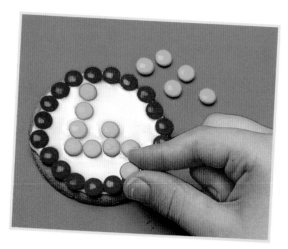

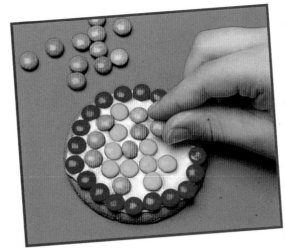

5 Press coloured sweets into the wet icing around the edge of the biscuit. Use a different colour to create a number in the middle.

6 Fill in the spaces around the number with another colour. Leave the biscuit until the icing is set.

FURTHER IDEAS

Why not mosaic your name on top of your birthday cake, or decorate some biscuits with simple shapes.

Grecian Coaster

The Greeks and Romans used small clay tiles to make their mosaics. In this project mosaic tiles are made using air-drying clay. The rolled out clay is soft enough to cut with a knife and most of the pieces are either squares or triangles, so the design can only have straight edges. When the clay is dry, it is painted with traditional Greek colours and the coaster is then sealed with PVA glue to protect it.

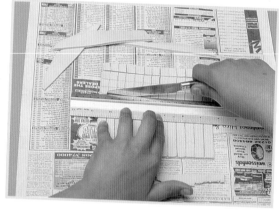

1 Cover your work surface with newspaper. Take a ball of clay, roughly the size of a tennis ball, and roll it out to a thickness of between 0.5cm and 0.8cm (¼in and ³/₈in).

2 Trim off the edges of the clay with a knife, using a ruler as a guide. Cut vertical lines approximately 1cm (½in) apart. Cut horizontal lines in the same way to form small clay squares.

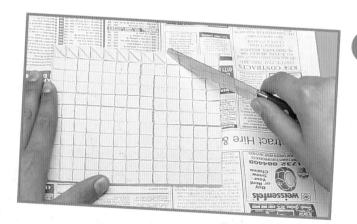

3 Cut a few of the squares diagonally to make triangles. Leave the clay to dry for two days.

Knives can be sharp. Ask an adult to help you cut the clay.

Use a small paintbrush and different colours to paint the squares and triangles.

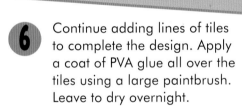

5 Cut out a piece of thick card roughly 11cm (4¼in) square. Using the design shown on page 80 as a guide, start to build up the mosaic design. Secure the tiles with PVA glue and work line by line.

6 Continue adding lines of tiles to complete the design. Apply a coat of PVA glue all over the tiles using a large paintbrush. Leave to dry overnight.

Note When PVA glue is dry, it can be very difficult to remove, so wear an apron or old shirt to protect your clothes.

FURTHER IDEAS
You can make matching place mats and pot stands using this technique.

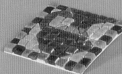

Seaside Pebble Frame

Small pebbles are great for making mosaics. You can sometimes find coloured ones on the beach, but you could paint the pebbles yourself if you could not find any. I have used white pebbles about the size of a pea and very small pebbles that have been painted after they have been glued down. Pearlescent paint has been used for a shimmering effect, which makes the picture frame look more colourful, but you can use any colour. Choose a frame with a very wide and flat border to give you plenty of space for your design, and use it to display your own drawing, painting or photograph.

YOU WILL NEED

Plain wooden frame
Selection of small pebbles
Newspaper • Carbon paper
Tracing paper • Masking tape
Pencil • Water-based paint
Paintbrush
PVA glue

 Transfer the patterns shown on page 81 on to your frame. Draw some waves in the background and then paint them, working from the top to the bottom.

 Apply PVA glue around the edge of the starfish, over the fish's body and around the edge of the fish's tail.

 Sprinkle very small pebbles over the wet glue to decorate the starfish and fish. Leave to dry for at least fifteen minutes.

4 Tip the frame over a piece of newspaper to remove excess pebbles. These can be saved and used for another project.

5 Paint the small pebbles on the fish and the starfish in colours of your choice.

6 Apply glue to the centre of the starfish. Add stripes of glue to the fish's body and tail, and lines of glue following the shape of the waves. Press larger pebbles into the glue, then leave to dry overnight.

FURTHER IDEAS
Cover the top of a box, or make decorative pebble pictures using this technique.

Celestial Pot

All sorts of materials can be used to create a mosaic. Here broken eggshells are glued on to a plain terracotta plant pot. The theme is the sky above – one side shows a sun, the other a moon and star. For a small pot like this you will need the shells of three eggs. If your pot is larger, you will need more. Use the completed pot for an indoor plant, as the mosaic will not be weatherproof.

 Wash the eggshells in warm water then place them on newspaper. Leave to dry.

2 Break the eggshells carefully into large pieces, then paint them with different colours. Leave to dry.

3 Transfer the patterns shown on page 81 on to your pot. Apply PVA glue to one of the areas of the design.

 Break the eggshells into smaller pieces. Firmly press one of the pieces on to the wet glue to break the shell up further.

5 Use a cocktail stick to push the pieces of eggshell apart, leaving small gaps in between.

6 Continue applying different colours to your design. Finish by filling in around the design with more eggshells and leave to dry.

FURTHER IDEAS

Create a beautiful jewellery box by decorating a plain wooden box with brightly coloured eggshells.

Aztec Book Cover

This book cover is inspired by the wonderful colours of the Aztecs. You can transform a cheap, plain, bound notebook easily with the bold geometric pattern. Detailed mosaic designs can take many hours to complete, but here the design is very quick, as the mosaic is created on a printing block that is then used to print a pattern over and over again. You can use many colours on this block and print instant designs.

YOU WILL NEED
Plain book
High-density foam
Thick card • Scissors
Water-based paint
Paintbrush • PVA glue
Cord • Bead

Cut high-density foam into small squares and triangles, using the design on page 81 as a rough guide.

2 Cut out a square of thick card, roughly the size of the design. Glue the foam pieces on to the card using PVA glue, following the lines of the design, to create a printing block. Leave to dry.

3 Apply a thin layer of paint to the foam squares and triangles using a small paintbrush and colours of your choice.

4 Press the printing block on to the front of your book.

5 Repeat, applying more paint each time. Complete a stripe down one side of the book. Leave to dry.

6 Loop a length of cord around the book, then thread a tightly-fitting bead through to secure it.

FURTHER IDEAS

Create your own mosaic design using different shapes, then stamp the design on to a picture frame.

Patterns

You can trace the patterns on these pages straight from the book (step 1). Alternatively, you can make them larger or smaller on a photocopier if you wish, and then follow steps 2–4.

Ask an adult to help you enlarge the patterns on a photocopier.

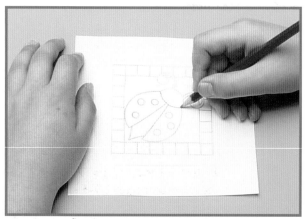

1 Place a piece of tracing paper over the pattern, then tape it down with small pieces of masking tape. Trace around the outline using a soft pencil.

2 Place carbon paper face down on the surface you want to transfer the design on to. Place the tracing or photocopy over the top and tape it in place.

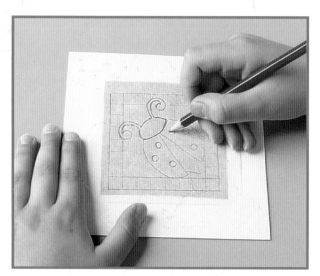

3 Trace over the outline with a pencil.

4 Remove the tracing paper and carbon paper to reveal the transferred image.

Patterns for the Insect Greetings Cards
featured on pages 58–59.

Patterns for the Knight in Armour
Picture featured on pages 62–63.

Pattern for the African Mask
featured on pages 60–61.

Pattern for the Indian Elephant
Shoebag featured on pages 64–65.

Pattern for the Egyptian Eagle Necklace
featured on pages 66–67.

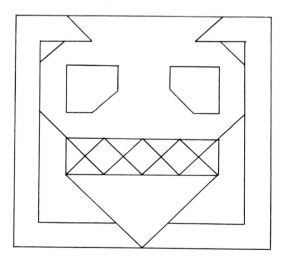

Pattern for the Grecian Coaster
featured on pages 70–71.

Patterns for the Celestial Pot featured on pages 74–75.

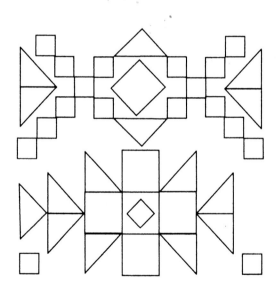

Patterns for the Seaside Pebble Frame featured on pages 72–73.

Pattern for the Aztec Book Cover featured on pages 76–77.

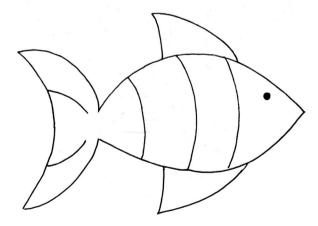

Papier Mâché

by Judy Balchin

Papier Mâché is a French term which means 'chewed or mashed paper'. It was first invented in China in the first part of the second century. The Chinese discovered that it was possible to make many items out of papier mâché – they created pots and even warrior helmets which they then covered with a varnish to make them hard-wearing and durable. Over time, mankind became more and more ambitious, and by the seventeenth century even a church was being built using papier mâché! In the following century, a man called Charles Ducrest drew up plans for making tables, bookcases and even houses, boats and bridges using either papier mâché on its own, or wood or iron structures covered in papier mâché.

Although you will not be making churches, houses or boats in this section, you will be able to have lots of fun with papier mâché – from making a simple photograph frame to modelling a cat. I have taken the inspiration for the items from past civilisations. You will be taken on a journey to discover Celtic and Indian decoration, Native American, Mexican and Gothic design, Egyptian, Aztec, Roman and African art.

There are two main ways of making papier mâché: layering and pulping. You will be using both methods in the projects in this section, sometimes combining both on one piece. Each project shows you a different way of using papier mâché and suggests how you can decorate your pieces.

If you are interested in recycling rubbish, then this section is definitely for you. Old newspapers, cardboard tubing and sweet wrappers are just a few of the things that you will be working with, so start hoarding! Before you throw anything away, ask yourself if it could be used in a papier mâché project. An old plastic bottle or cardboard box can spark off an amazing idea, so keep your eyes open. In particular, watch out for coloured papers, beads, feathers, string and foil papers . . . in fact anything that could be used to decorate your creations.

We all like to make things, but to make something totally unique has a special meaning. As you become more confident using papier mâché, I am sure you will come up with lots of your own ideas and designs. Be bold, experiment, but most of all, have lots of fun.

Opposite *Many people think that papier mâché is used only by children to make simple and inexpensive items like masks. However, this richly decorated box, called a casket, was made from papier mâché in the 1770s. It must have been bought by a very wealthy or important person, because it would have cost a great deal of money to decorate it so beautifully.*

Techniques

Papier mâché is not a difficult craft, but it is worth reading through this techniques section carefully before you begin the projects.

Note Papier mâché is messy so it is best to cover your workspace with a large piece of newspaper. Alternatively, use polythene – this can be wiped down and used again.

Transferring a design on to cardboard

Patterns are provided at the end of the section. These can be enlarged on a photocopier. Cut around the photocopied pattern, then lay it on thin card or single corrugated cardboard and run round the edge with a pencil. Cut around the line with scissors.

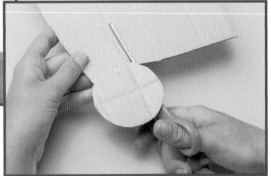

> **!**
>
> Double corrugated cardboard is much tougher than single, and it needs to be cut with a craft knife. Ask an adult to do this for you as craft knives are very sharp.

Preventing warping

Sometimes, papier mâché pieces made from a cardboard base can warp during the drying process. To prevent this, always give your base cardboard shape a coat of slightly diluted PVA glue.

Paste both sides of the cardboard then leave to dry naturally on a cooling rack, turning occasionally so that it dries evenly. When completely dry, the cardboard can be layered with newspaper strips (see opposite).

Note When PVA glue is dry, it can be very difficult to remove so wear an apron or old shirt to protect your clothes.

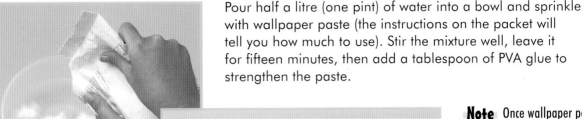

Mixing up the paste

Pour half a litre (one pint) of water into a bowl and sprinkle with wallpaper paste (the instructions on the packet will tell you how much to use). Stir the mixture well, leave it for fifteen minutes, then add a tablespoon of PVA glue to strengthen the paste.

Note Once wallpaper paste has been made up, it can be stored in a bowl fitted with an airtight lid or sealed with clingfilm. It will last for several days if kept in the fridge.

Layering with newspaper strips

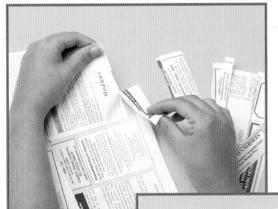

Layering involves pasting strips of newspaper with a mixture of wallpaper paste and PVA glue, and then sticking them on to a base. When dry, the pieces will be strong but light, and ready for decorating.

Tear small strips of newspaper for small structures, and larger strips for bigger items. Use your fingers to smear paste on to the strips of paper then press them on to your base so that they overlap each other. Smooth the strips down as you work.

Note Complete one layer at a time. You will be told how many layers to apply for each project. To help you keep count of the number of layers you have worked, you can apply one layer of coloured newspaper, then one layer of black and white and so on.

Using paper pulp

Papier mâché pulp can be bought from art shops. It is a powdered paper which is mixed with water to create a modelling material. You can also make your own, as shown here. Once you have mixed up the pulp, it can be stored in a polythene bag in the fridge until needed.

1 Tear enough small pieces of newspaper to fill a mug when packed tightly.

2 Place the pieces of newspaper in a bowl and cover with hot water. Leave to soak for three hours.

3 Transfer the soaked paper into a colander or sieve. Squeeze the pieces together so that the water runs out and the paper forms a mash.

4 Put the mash into a bowl and add a tablespoon of PVA glue and a tablespoon of wallpaper paste mixture (see page 9).

5 Mix everything together with your fingers.

Note When you have completed a pulped papier mâché project, leave it to dry naturally. The pulp shrinks as it dries and sometimes creates small splits or cracks in the surface. These can be disguised by smearing a little more paper pulp into them and allowing this to dry again.

Priming and painting

Priming means preparing a surface so that it can then be decorated with coloured paint. Use white emulsion paint to do this. You may need two coats to cover the newspaper print completely. Allow the first coat to dry before applying the second.

The projects in this book are decorated with acrylic paint as it covers well, is hard-wearing and does not need to be varnished. Once the white primer is dry, paint your finished object in colours of your choice.

Note All items painted with poster paint should be protected with a coat of varnish – you can use diluted PVA glue for this. If you do use poster paints, mix it with a little PVA glue before you apply it. This will prevent the paint from smearing when you varnish it.

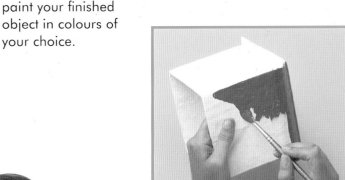

Celtic Goblet

Celtic craftsmen were well-known for their metal work. The goblet in this project is made to look like metal, but it is actually made out of an old plastic drinks bottle. The surface is covered with pulp to create a textured surface which looks like beaten metal. It is decorated with metallic paint and glass droplets to create a container that is truly fit for a king! Remember that this goblet is purely decorative and can not be used to drink out of.

YOU WILL NEED

Plastic drinks bottle
Single corrugated cardboard
Paper pulp • Glass droplets
Metallic acrylic paint
Paintbrush • Palette • PVA glue
Scissors • Masking tape
Newspaper

2 Cut a circle of single corrugated cardboard approximately 6.5cm (2½in) in diameter. Use masking tape to attach the cardboard circle to the top of the bottle.

1 Cut off the top third of a plastic drinks bottle.

3 Cover the outside of the plastic bottle and the cardboard base with a layer of pulp.

Note The pulp may dry on your fingers as you work. Keep a bowl of water next to you so that you can wet your fingers occasionally to stop this from happening.

4

Neaten the rim of the goblet by pressing the pulp onto the plastic edge.

5

While the pulp is still wet, put a blob of PVA glue on the back of eight glass droplets and then press them firmly into the pulp around the goblet. Leave to dry for forty-eight hours.

6 Paint the inside and outside of the goblet with metallic acrylic paint.

FURTHER IDEAS
Decorate your goblet using buttons or small pebbles instead of glass droplets.

Indian Frame

The shape of this Indian frame was inspired by the domed roof of the Taj Mahal, a beautiful tomb in India which was built by a Mogul Emperor for his wife. The decoration for the frame is based on Indian saris – these are made of brightly coloured cloth and metallic threads. I have used sweet wrappers and metallic paint in this project to transform a plain piece of cardboard into a frame to treasure.

YOU WILL NEED

Coloured foil sweet wrappers
Double corrugated cardboard
Thin card • Newspaper
Wallpaper paste • PVA glue • Paste brush
Metallic and coloured acrylic paint
Sponge • Palette • Pencil
Scissors • Craft knife • String
Masking tape

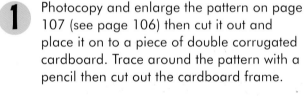

(!) Double corrugated cardboard needs to be cut with a craft knife. Ask an adult to do this for you as craft knives are very sharp.

2 Paste both sides of the cardboard frame with PVA glue diluted with a little water. Leave to dry. Apply two layers of pasted newspaper strips to the front then leave to dry for a couple of hours.

1 Photocopy and enlarge the pattern on page 107 (see page 106) then cut it out and place it on to a piece of double corrugated cardboard. Trace around the pattern with a pencil then cut out the cardboard frame.

3 Tear foil sweet wrappers into irregular shapes. Paste the back of each piece with PVA glue then press them on to the cardboard frame. Cover the front and the edges. Overlap the foil pieces on to the back. Leave to dry.

4 Pour a little metallic acrylic paint on to a palette. Dip a piece of sponge into the paint then dab it on to the outer and inner edges of the frame. Leave to dry.

5

Paint the back of the frame in a colour of your choice. Leave to dry. Cut out a piece of thin card, slightly bigger than the opening in the frame. Cut a wide 'v' shape in the top of the card. Tape the card over the opening, leaving the top un-taped – this will create a pocket for your picture or photograph.

6 Tape a loop of string to the back of the frame for hanging, then leave to dry. Insert your picture or photograph.

FURTHER IDEAS
Create a different effect by decorating your frame with torn pieces of coloured tissue paper.

Native American Headdress

YOU WILL NEED
Large and small feathers
Coloured beads • String
Single corrugated cardboard
Paper pulp • Newspaper • Balloon
Small bowl • White emulsion paint
Coloured acrylic paint • Palette
Paintbrush • Sponge • Scissors
Pencil • Masking tape

A war bonnet decorated with eagle feathers is the mark of an experienced and respected warrior. The colourful headdress in this project is decorated with brightly coloured paints, beads and feathers. When you wear it, you will feel like the chief of your tribe.

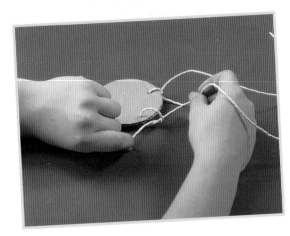

1 Use scissors to cut out the shape of the headdress shown on page 107 from single corrugated cardboard (see page 90). Pierce two holes in each disc shape with the end of a paintbrush. Thread a length of string through each hole and tie to secure.

2 Cover one side of the cardboard with pulp. Leave the corrugations along the top of the cardboard shape uncovered as you will later stick feathers into these. Add a little more pulp over the circular disk shapes. Roll out a sausage of pulp and press this along the headdress to create a raised zig-zag decoration.

3 Blow up a balloon to approximately the same size as your head. Use masking tape to attach the balloon to a small bowl. Tie the headdress around the balloon and leave to dry for forty-eight hours.

4

Prime the headdress with white emulsion. When dry, decorate with zig-zags and dots of coloured acrylic paint.

FURTHER IDEAS
Paint the headband with earthy colours and use natural feathers for a different effect.

5 Sponge the lengths of string with coloured paint. When dry, thread the strings at the bottom with coloured beads. Leave the strings at the side un-beaded, so you can tie it around your head.

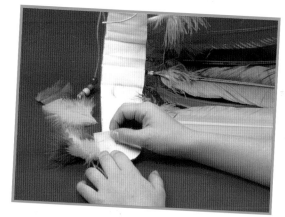

6 Push large coloured feathers into the holes along the top of the corrugated card, then tape two small feathers down each side.

Mexican Bowl

The inspiration for this bright little bowl comes from Mexico. In fact, the art of pot-making originated from the Mexican area as there was a lot of clay in the soil. Mexicans use bright colours and geometric designs to decorate their craft work. In this project, paper pulp is used to make a textured bowl. You can use any bowl as a mould for this project (ceramic, plastic or glass) and it does not matter what size it is. Remember that the finished papier mâché bowl is intended to be decorative – you cannot eat out of it!

YOU WILL NEED

Selection of coloured beads
60cm (24in) of leather thong
Bowl • Clingfilm • Paper pulp
Newspaper • White emulsion paint
Coloured acrylic paint
Paintbrush • Palette
Cooling rack

Line the inside of a bowl with clingfilm. Press paper pulp into the bowl with your fingers. When it is about 1cm (½in) thick, smooth the surface with your fingers.

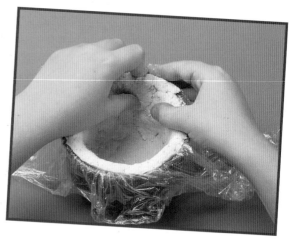

2 Use the end of a paintbrush to make holes around the bowl. Try to make the spaces between the holes roughly equal. Leave to dry for three hours.

3 Carefully lift the pulp shell out of the bowl using the clingfilm. Place on a cooling rack then leave to dry for at least twenty-four hours.

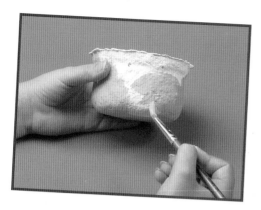

4

Prime the bowl with two coats of white emulsion paint. Leave to dry. Paint the outside of the bowl with coloured acrylic paint. Leave to dry.

5 Paint the inside of the bowl a different colour. Leave to dry.

6

Tie a knot in the length of thong and attach three beads. Thread it through one of the holes in the bowl. Tie a knot on the inside then cut off the end of the thong. Repeat around the bowl using the rest of the thong.

FURTHER IDEAS
Use a needle and cotton to thread dried melon or sunflower seeds on to your bowl.

Gothic Mirror

Gothic architecture sparked off the idea for this mirror. If you visit an old church and look at the pointed arches and carved stonework you will soon see the similarities. The mirror in this project is created using a mirror tile on a cardboard base. I have covered the cardboard with paper pulp to create a stone brickwork effect.

YOU WILL NEED

Mirror tile
Double corrugated cardboard
Paper pulp • Newspaper • PVA glue
Wallpaper paste • Paste brush
Natural-coloured acrylic paint
Paintbrush • Palette • Ruler
Masking tape • Soft cloth
Cooling rack

1 Cut out the frame shape shown on page 106 from double corrugated card (see page 90). Coat both sides with diluted PVA glue then allow to dry on a cooling rack.

2 Apply two layers of pasted newspaper strips to the front and back of the frame. Leave to dry for four hours.

3 Apply PVA glue to the back of the mirror and then press it into place on the frame.

4 Press paper pulp on to the front and edges of the cardboard frame. Smooth the pulp with your fingers as you work.

While the pulp is still wet, use the long edge of a ruler to press horizontal lines into the pulp. Use the short edge of the ruler to create vertical lines. This will give the effect of stone brickwork. Leave to dry for forty-eight hours.

6 Paint the frame with natural-coloured paint then polish the mirror with a soft cloth.

Note If the frame starts to warp while the paper pulp is drying, place something heavy on the mirror tile – this will help flatten the frame.

FURTHER IDEAS
Make the mirror frame Norman rather than Gothic by cutting out a rounded arch.

Egyptian Cat

The Ancient Egyptians worshipped the cat goddess, Bastet, and made bronze cat figures dedicated to her. Bastet represented the power of the sun to ripen crops. This project uses a plastic bottle and a polystyrene ball as a base for re-creating Bastet. Pulp is used to model her features and, once painted, she is sponged with metallic paint to make her look like a real goddess.

YOU WILL NEED

Plastic drinks bottle
Polystyrene ball • Ribbon
Paper pulp • Newspaper
Coloured and metallic acrylic paint
Palette • Sponge • Paintbrush
PVA glue • Paste brush
Masking tape

1. Remove the bottle cap and place the polystyrene ball on top of the bottle. Tape the ball into place with long strips of masking tape. Press the tape flat on to the bottle to create a smooth finish.

2. Cover the polystyrene ball with a layer of paper pulp. Build up the nose then model two triangles of pulp to create the ears. Smooth the pulp with your fingers as you work.

3. Work down the bottle, covering it with pulp. Build up the front legs and feet then the hind legs and feet using pulp. Neaten the base of the bottle then leave to dry for two days.

4. Paint the cat with coloured acrylic paint. Leave to dry. Paint in the eyes and nose in a darker colour.

5 Paint in the collar with coloured and metallic paint then leave to dry. Glue on a strip of ribbon around the top of the collar.

6 Pour a little metallic paint on to a palette. Lightly sponge the cat all over.

FURTHER IDEAS

Look for a picture of the Egyptian god, Anubis, who is represented as a jackal. Try creating a model of its head.

Aztec Necklace

Aztec craftsmen made beautiful jewellery. They considered jade to be their most precious stone, but they also used onyx, rock crystal and turquoise. The necklace in this project is made out of pulp which has been decorated with string, foil and metallic paint.

YOU WILL NEED

Foil • String
Paper pulp • Newspaper
Clingfilm • Cardboard
Coloured and metallic acrylic paint
Paintbrush • Sponge
PVA glue • Paste brush
Masking tape
Cooling rack

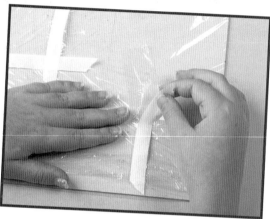

1 Tape a piece of clingfilm over a piece of card so that it is stretched tight.

2 Model a rectangle and a triangle of pulp then press each shape on to the clingfilm, flattening them with your fingers.

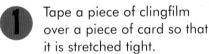

3 Press string into each pulp shape to create swirling patterns.

4 Use the end of a paintbrush to create two holes in the top corners and one in the bottom of the rectangular piece. Make one hole at the top of the triangle. Leave to dry for an hour. Carefully remove the shapes from the clingfilm then lay them on a cooling rack and leave to dry for a further twelve hours.

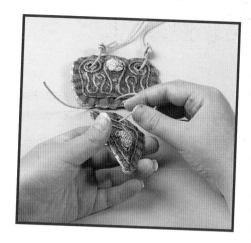

Sponge a length of
string with metallic
paint. Cut off a short
piece and use this to
link the rectangle and
triangle together. Tie two
longer pieces of string
on to the rectangle so
that you can do the
necklace up.

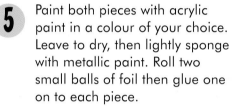

5 Paint both pieces with acrylic
paint in a colour of your choice.
Leave to dry, then lightly sponge
with metallic paint. Roll two
small balls of foil then glue one
on to each piece.

FURTHER IDEAS
Model round pieces of
pulp and attach earring
clips to the back to make
earrings. Thread round
shapes with string to
create a bracelet.

Roman Box

Roman city houses were often plain on the outside, but on the inside they were painted with scenes from mythology or the countryside. Romans covered their floors with mosaics (pictures and patterns made up from small pieces of stone). This project shows you how to make a simple mosaic box using cardboard, paint and a potato stamp. I have varnished the finished piece with diluted PVA glue to make it look shiny.

1 Cut out four 12cm (4¾in) and two 14cm (5½in) squares from single corrugated cardboard. Now cut out one 11cm (4¼in) and one 4cm (1½in) square. Tape the four 12cm (4¾in) squares together with masking tape to form the sides of the box. Tape one 14cm (5½in) square to one end to create a base.

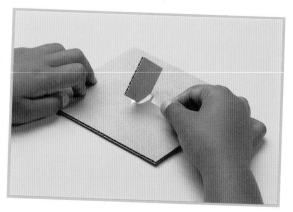

2 To make a lid, glue the 11cm (4¼in) square to the centre of the remaining 14cm (5½in) square. Leave to dry. Turn over and pierce through the centre of the larger square with the end of a paintbrush. Apply a blob of glue to the hole then push a corner of the 4cm (1½in) square into the hole. Secure with small pieces of masking tape.

3 Coat the box and lid with diluted PVA glue. Leave to dry then apply two layers of pasted newspaper strips to the box. Leave to dry for four hours. Prime the box with two coats of white emulsion. Leave to dry.

4 Cut a 1cm (½in) wide chip shape from a potato. Dab it into acrylic paint then use it to stamp the sides of the box.

!

It is best to cut the potato on a chopping board. Get an adult to help you do this as vegetable knives are very sharp.

5 Stamp three rows of squares around the lid then paint the handle.

6 Paint the rim of the base and the inside of the box. Leave to dry then apply a coat of diluted PVA glue to varnish the outside of the box and the lid.

FURTHER IDEAS

Cut triangular and rectangular shaped potato shapes and use these to stamp a different design on to your box.

African Pencil Pot

The inspiration for this project comes from African drums. I have used cardboard tubing to recreate the cylindrical drum shapes and have decorated the pencil pot with colours typical of African art. It is best to use different sizes of cardboard tubing. You can make a simple pencil pot using just a few tubes, or you can use lots to create a more complicated one.

1

Cut out five different lengths of cardboard tubing. Tape the tubes together, making sure that the bases are level. Place the tubes on a piece of thin card and draw around the bases. Cut around this shape then attach it to the bottom of the tubes using masking tape.

2 Apply two layers of newspaper strips over the pencil pot then allow to dry for four hours.

3

Prime the pencil pot with white emulsion paint then leave to dry. Apply a coat of coloured acrylic paint. When dry, paint coloured lines down each tube and a zig-zag border around the base. Leave to dry.

5 Paint a dark border around the base of the pencil pot, and add small triangles within the larger coloured ones.

6 Paint a dark band around the top of each tube then allow to dry. Finally, use the same colour to paint the inside of the tubes.

4 Dip a toothbrush into diluted acrylic paint, then hold it over the pencil pot and pull back the bristles with your finger. This will create a spattered paint effect. Wash your hands immediately afterwards.

FURTHER IDEAS
Create a completely different look by decorating with spots and stars instead of stripes and triangles.

Patterns

You can photocopy the patterns on these
pages and then transfer the designs on to
cardboard (see page 84). Use them the size
that they appear here, or make them larger
or smaller on a photocopier if you wish.

!
Get an adult to help you photocopy the patterns.

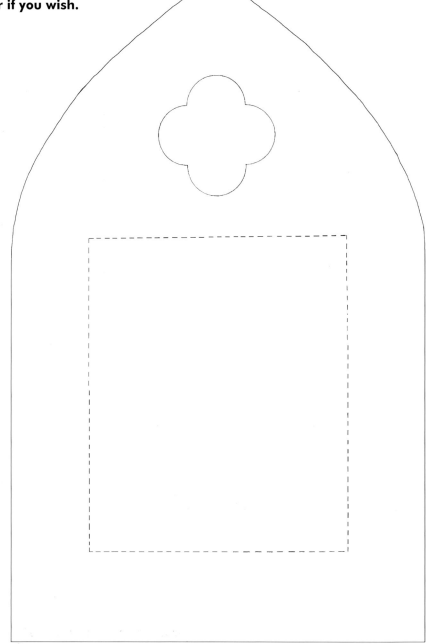

*Pattern for the Gothic Mirror
featured on pages 96–97.*

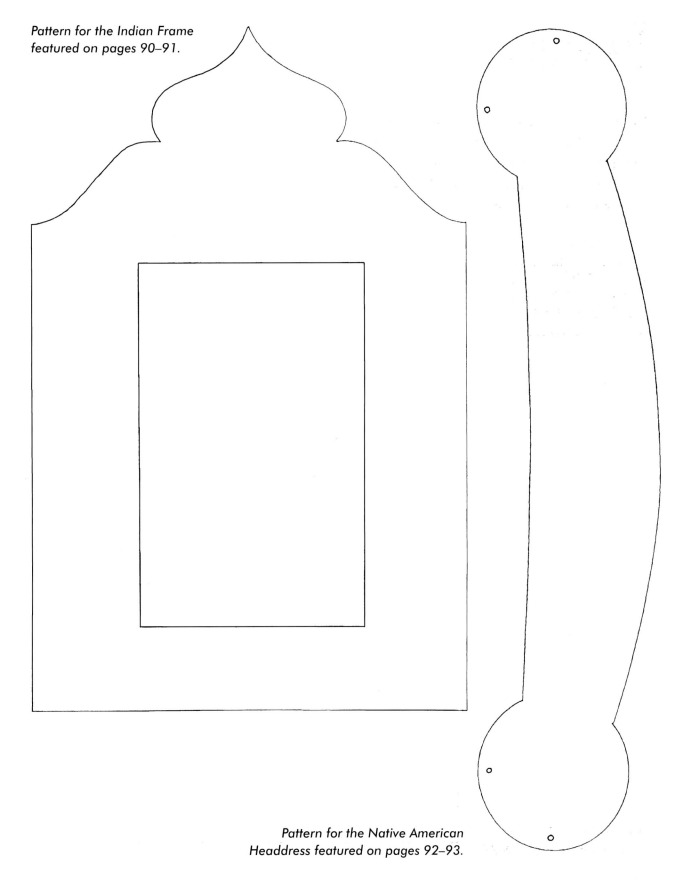

Pattern for the Indian Frame featured on pages 90–91.

Pattern for the Native American Headdress featured on pages 92–93.

Origami

by Clive Stevens

It is generally believed that paper was invented in China around the first century AD, and the Chinese soon began to fold the new material into decorative shapes. When paper was introduced to Japan in the sixth century AD by Buddhist monks, it rapidly became an important part of their culture. Paper was used as part of many religious ceremonies, and even as a building material. It was the Japanese who turned paper folding into an art, which in Japan is as important as painting and sculpture. Origami comes from the Japanese words for folding, *ori*, and paper, *kami*.

The Japanese passed on their paper folding designs by word of mouth; many were passed down from mother to daughter. In the early days, paper was too expensive to be used for fun, so paper folding was done only for important ceremonies. Paper butterflies were made to decorate the cups for *sake* (rice wine) used at Japanese weddings.

By the seventeenth century, paper had become less expensive, and origami had become a popular pastime in Japan. The first origami books with diagrams and instructions were published in the early eighteenth century.

Today, master paper folders can be found all over the world. Folding techniques have improved so much that they would have astounded the ancient Japanese who invented origami.

In this book, you will learn how to make good, crisp folds so that your paper will hold the right shapes. Follow the instructions carefully, and this is all you need to know to make some simple but very effective projects.

In origami, many different shapes can be made from a few simple bases. The Origami Bases chapter on pages 112–113 shows you how to make two of these bases, and once you have mastered folding these, you are ready to make some very impressive projects!

Don't worry if your folding doesn't work the first time. Go over the instructions and pictures again carefully, and you will soon find where you went wrong.

You hardly need any materials to do origami, and it is easy to become hooked. After a few tries, you will learn the folds off by heart, and then all you need is a piece of paper to produce impressive designs that will amaze your friends!

Opposite
This amazing origami beetle is only about 2.5cm (1in) long. It was designed and folded by the Italian paper folder, Alfredo Giunta.

Techniques

Folding in half

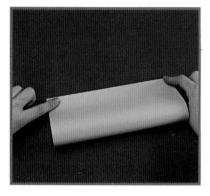

1 Fold the bottom corners upwards to meet the top corners. This will make a horizontal fold.

2 Make a crease in the middle. Press with your finger from the middle to the edge, then from the middle to the other edge. Make sure the corners stay together.

3 Reinforce the crease by pressing it with your fingernail.

Folding diagonally

Start with a square piece of paper. Lift up one corner and meet it up with the corner diagonally opposite to it. Make a crease in the middle of the paper and work out from the middle to the sides. This makes a diagonal fold.

Folding at an angle

Lay a strip of paper horizontally. Fold part of the strip downwards so that the edges of the strip make a right angle, like the corner of a square.

Reverse Folding (internal)

Reverse folding means that you push a fold until it folds in the opposite direction. A valley fold (which dips downwards) becomes a mountain fold (which points upwards), and vice versa. This internal reverse fold is used for the Flapping Bird project on pages 130–131.

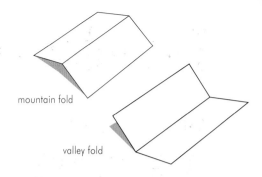

mountain fold

valley fold

1 Fold a square piece of paper in half diagonally. Fold the top corner down as shown and crease it sharply.

2 Open the paper up slightly. Pull the top point towards you. Reverse the mountain fold in the middle of the point, making it a valley fold.

3 Remake the diagonal fold and open it up to show the point with its valley fold.

Reverse Folding (external)

This type of external reverse fold is used for the Paper Penguin project on pages 118–119.

1 Take a square piece of paper and fold it diagonally. Fold down the top point as shown and crease firmly.

2 Open up with the diagonal mountain fold facing towards you. Fold the top point towards you. Reverse the fold in the middle of the point. Now remake the diagonal fold, so that the point comes down on the outside of the diagonal fold.

Origami Bases

Many origami designs come from a few simple bases. Here are two bases which can lead to all sorts of different projects.

Bird Base

This base is used to make the Flapping Bird project on page 130. Steps 1 to 3 also start off the Folded Flower project on page 126.

1 Take a square of paper. Fold the square diagonally. Crease it firmly and open. Fold on the other diagonal, crease and open. Turn the paper over so that your diagonal folds are mountain folds, as shown above.

2 Now fold up the bottom two corners to meet the top two corners and fold the paper in half horizontally. Crease, unfold, and then fold in half the other way to make a cross shape. Turn the paper over and place it as shown, so that the horizontal folds are mountain folds, and the diagonal folds are valley folds that dip down.

3

Hold the edges of a horizontal fold as shown. Move your hands in together until the paper forms a square. There should be two flaps on either side of the square as shown.

open end

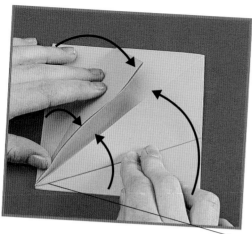

open end

 4 Fold the front flaps, bringing the edges in to the middle. Make sure the open end of the shape is at the bottom as shown.

open end

5 Turn over and repeat on the other side.

Rocket Base

This is used in the Space Rocket project on pages 128–129 and the Blow-up Box on pages 132–133.

 1

Start making the Bird Base, but only go as far as Step 2. Turn the paper over so that the diagonal folds are mountain folds and the horizontal folds are valley folds. Fold one of the diagonal folds and hold it by the corners. Push your hands downwards to form a triangle.

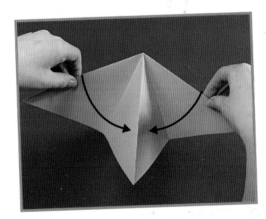

2

The triangle should have two flaps on either side, like the square made in step 3 of the Bird Base.

Note If your origami bases have not turned out right, check these things:
• Make sure your folds are sharply creased.
• If your diagonal folds are mountain folds, your horizontal folds should be valley folds.
• Make sure the open end of the shape is at the bottom.

Layered Fan

Many people have learnt to make a simple fan by folding a piece of paper into a concertina shape. This may have been your first introduction to paper folding! However, folding this way can lead to uneven folds and an untidy finished fan. This is an origami fan, made from basic valley and mountain folds. This method means that you fold the paper so that it is divided equally.

YOU WILL NEED

Three different coloured papers:
10 x 30cm (4 x 11¾in)
12 x 30cm (4¾ x 11¾in)
14 x 30cm (5½ x 11¾in)

1 Place all three pieces of paper together as shown. Fold them in half and unfold.

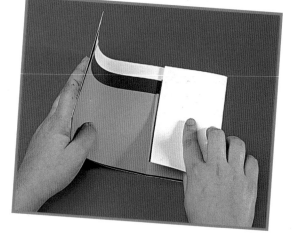

2 Fold the right and left edges in to the centre line.

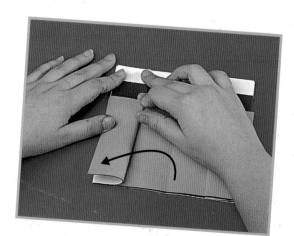

3 Take one of the edges that you have folded in to the middle, and fold it back to the new edge. Repeat the other side as shown.

 4

Fold in half, bringing the double outside edges together.

5 Fold the top flap back. Turn the paper over and repeat on the other side.

6 Open up and pinch at the bottom to form a multicoloured fan.

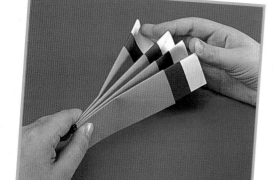

FURTHER IDEAS

Make fans from patterned origami paper, wrapping paper, or even beautiful Japanese handmade papers.

Secrets Folder

This handy folder is made using simple folds and also a tuck fold. It can be any size you want, from a tiny purse for loose change, to a folder like the one shown here, for larger secrets! Remember that the folder you end up with will be much smaller than the piece of paper you start with. You need to cut down an A2 size piece of paper to make a folder as big as the one shown in these photographs. What you hide in your secrets folder is up to you!

YOU WILL NEED
Coloured or patterned paper
30 x 50cm (12 x 20in)

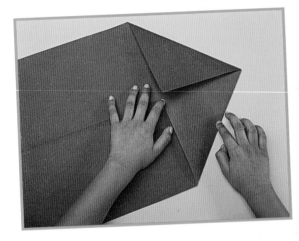

1 Place the paper, shiny side down and fold in half horizontally. Unfold. Fold the two top corners in to the centre line.

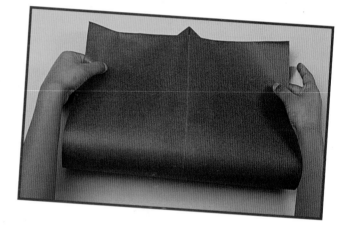

2 Fold the bottom edge up to the point at the top.

3 Now fold the outside edges in to the centre fold.

4

Fold the bottom edge to the top of the diagonal folds.

5 Tuck the flap into the front pocket.

6

Fold the point down to form the front flap of the secrets folder.

FURTHER IDEAS

Try using metallic or patterned papers, or decorate a piece of paper yourself using paints or felt tip pens before folding.

Paper Penguin

Origami paper with black on one side and white on the other works perfectly for this project. Using very few folds, you can create something that stands up like a real penguin. Penguins are some of the most sociable of all birds – they like to swim and feed in groups, so why not make a whole group of penguins and a paper pool for them to go fishing in?

YOU WILL NEED
One 10cm (4in) square piece of paper, black on one side and white on the other.

1 Take your square piece of paper. Fold it diagonally in half with the white on the inside to make a crease, then unfold. Turn the paper over. Take a corner at one end of the diagonal fold, and fold it up 2½cm (1in) as shown. Crease sharply.

2 Reverse the diagonal fold so that the white is on the outside, to make the shape shown.

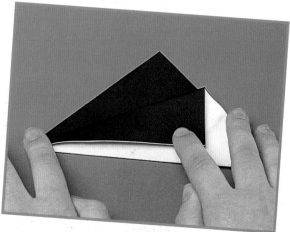

3 Fold the top point down to 1½cm (½in) from the bottom fold, and crease. Turn the paper over and repeat. This step is like making the wings on a paper aeroplane.

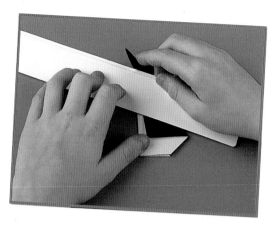

Place a ruler over the shape and fold the point down against the edge of a ruler at the angle shown. Remove the ruler and crease.

5

Open up slightly and pull the point towards you, making an external reverse fold as shown on page 111. This will make the penguin's head point downwards.

6 Crease the penguin again so that it is completely flat and open it up to reveal the finished penguin.

FURTHER IDEAS
Make a group of penguins in different colours and sizes, and maybe a paper pool for them to dive into!

Picture Frame

This simple origami frame is the perfect place to put one of your drawings, or a favourite photograph. Use thin card instead of paper, as this will make a stronger frame. The picture that goes inside this frame can be up to 14.5cm (5¾in) square, but don't forget that only a 10.5cm (4in) square in the middle will show.

YOU WILL NEED
Square of brightly coloured thin card,
30 x 30cm
(11¾ x 11¾in)

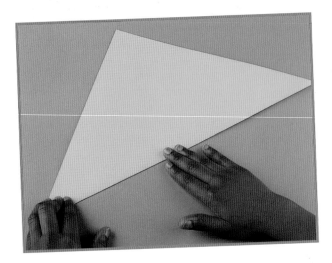

1 Fold the square diagonally corner to corner.

2 Open up and repeat on the other two corners.

3 Open up again. Your diagonal folds should be valley folds. Fold one corner down to the centre. Fold the other corners down to the centre.

 4

Turn the paper over and again fold all corners down to the centre.

 5

Turn the base over and fold all the points out to their corners.

6

Measure your picture frame. Draw a picture or find a photograph this size, remembering that the corners will be hidden by the frame. Slide the picture into the frame.

FURTHER IDEAS

Fold only as far as step 4 to make a drinks mat. Cover the mat in plastic to make it spill-proof.

Japanese Card

People have been sending one another greetings cards for hundreds of years. The first ones celebrated holidays or religious festivals, but nowadays they are sent for all kinds of reasons. Handmade cards are even more special than shop-bought ones. This Japanese greetings card has contrasting shades of the same colour to make it eye-catching. You open the flaps and write your message inside.

YOU WILL NEED
Two pieces of contrasting coloured paper, 23.5cm (9in) square

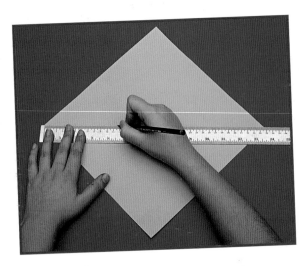

1 Put the squares of paper one on top of the other. Measure across the diagonal and mark it in to thirds of 11cm (4¼in) each.

2 Fold the corner along the diagonal. Fold on your first mark, up to your second mark.

3 Unfold. Turn the paper round and fold the opposite corner up to your first fold.

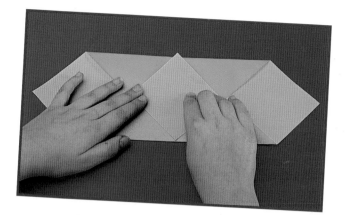

4 Fold one corner up to the top edge. Take the opposite corner out from under the top flap and fold it down to the bottom edge.

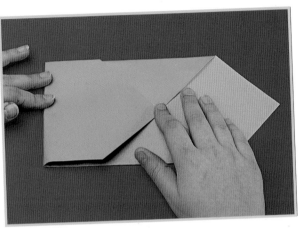

5 Fold one side in to cover the central light-coloured square. Fold the other side in as well.

6 Fold the triangular flap out to the outside edge and repeat the other side.

FURTHER IDEAS
Create a traditional Japanese card from glossy black and red paper.

Obi Bookmark

This traditional folding technique looks like the sash or *obi* worn round a Japanese kimono. Use bright, contrasting colours to give your bookmark a modern look. You need long strips of paper to start with, so make sure you cut them from an A2 size sheet. Once you have mastered the overlapping technique, you will be able to make a variety of bookmarks in different lengths and colours. They make the ideal gift for a friend who likes reading.

YOU WILL NEED
Two strips of paper in contrasting colours, 54 x 3cm (21¼ x 1¼in)
Scissors
Ruler

26cm (10¼in) from left

Put one strip on top of the other. Fold the strips at an angle, as shown on page 110. The fold should come 26cm (10¼in) from the left-hand end of the strips.

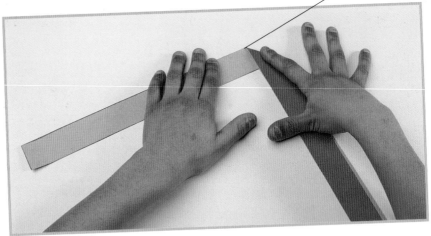

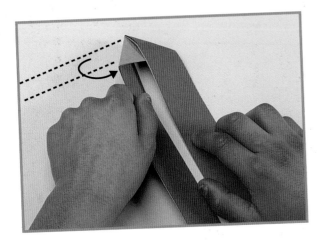

Fold the left-hand strips under at an angle. The strips should run parallel with the right-hand strips.

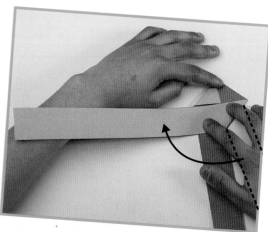

Fold the right-hand strip at an angle as shown.

124

 4

Slip the top right-hand strips under the left-hand strips.

5 Repeat steps 2, 3 and 4. Carry on doing this until four squares have been formed.

6 Fold the excess under neatly or trim the ends using scissors.

FURTHER IDEAS

Use contrasting papers: weave textured and glossy paper or patterned and plain paper together.

Folded Flower

This origami flower starts out as a square, but with a few folds it turns in to a flower shape, and curling the ends of the petals gives it a natural beauty. Why not make lots of flowers in different colours, with straws or pipe cleaners for stems. Then you can arrange them in a vase or bouquet.

1 Fold the square diagonally. Crease it firmly and open up. Then fold it on the other diagonal and open up the paper as shown above. Your diagonal folds should be mountain folds.

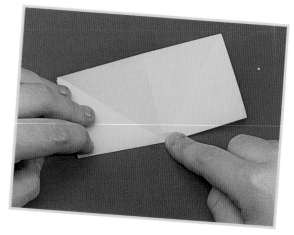

2 Fold up the bottom two corners to meet the top two corners and make a horizontal fold. Crease, unfold and then fold the paper in half the other way. Now your horizontal folds are mountain folds and your diagonal folds are valley folds.

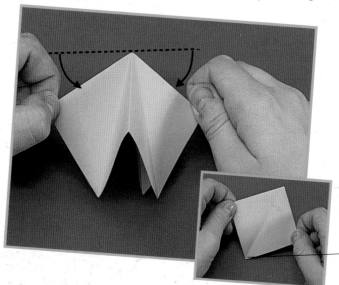

3 Hold the ends of a horizontal fold with both hands as shown, moving your hands together until the paper forms a square with two flaps on each side.

open end

126

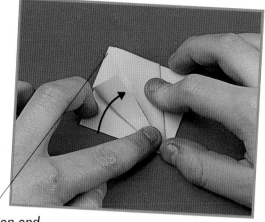

open end

4 Turn the square the other way up so that the open point is at the top. Fold the front flaps as shown, bringing the edges into the middle. Crease firmly. Turn over and repeat on the other side.

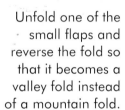

5 Unfold one of the small flaps and reverse the fold so that it becomes a valley fold instead of a mountain fold. Repeat with the other three flaps.

open end

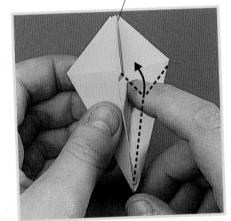

6 Open out the flower. Using a pencil or a cocktail stick, roll the tops of all four points down to create the natural curl of a petal.

FURTHER IDEAS
Make much bigger flowers, and then make smaller flowers without curling the petals. These make centres for the big flowers.

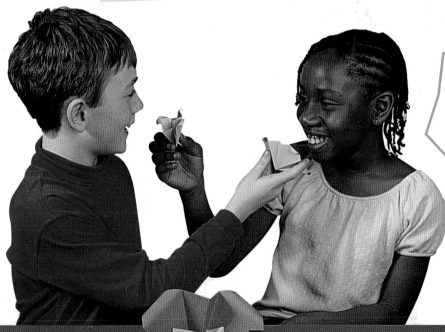

Space Rocket

This rocket is made from silver metallic origami paper that is white on the other side. It has legs that point outwards at an angle, so that it can stand up on its own, ready for take-off! Once you have mastered the Rocket Base, you are ready to fold and launch your own rocket – or maybe a whole fleet of spaceships!

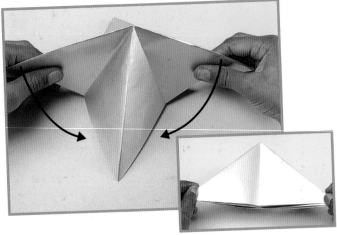

YOU WILL NEED
Square of metallic paper,
21 x 21cm (8¼ x 8¼in)

1 First make the Rocket Base as shown on page 113. Make sure that the shiny side of the paper is on the outside when you make your diagonal folds and on the inside when you make the horizontal folds. Hold the edges of a diagonal mountain fold and bring your hands in to make the triangle shape shown, with two flaps on each side.

2 Fold the outer edges in to the middle as shown. Turn the paper over and repeat.

3 Fold the outer corners to the middle. Turn the paper over and repeat on the other side.

4

Fold the bottom
points out at an
angle as shown.

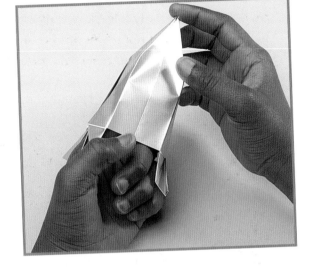

5

Turn over
and repeat.

6

Carefully open up the
rocket by placing your
finger inside.

FURTHER IDEAS

Leave the rocket flat as in
step 5 and glue it on to a
greetings card.

Flapping Bird

This bird is a variation of the traditional origami crane, a bird that is a Japanese symbol for peace. The crane is also the symbol for many international origami societies. This version is simpler, but if you hold it in the right place, it actually flaps its wings. Once you have got the hang of the Bird Base shown on pages 112–113, you will be ready to fold this impressive project to amaze all your friends.

YOU WILL NEED
Square piece of paper,
24.5cm² (9¾in²)

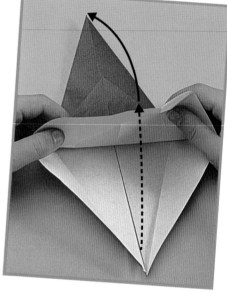

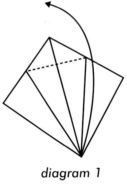

diagram 1

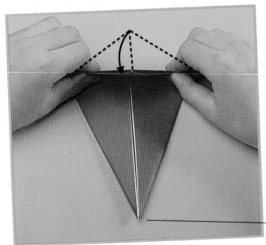

— *open end*

1 Start with the Bird Base, with the open end at the bottom. Fold the smaller triangle down, crease and fold back to its original position.

2 Unfold the side flaps as in diagram 1. Fold the bottom point up, covering the small triangle from step 1. Fold the point right up to the top, reversing the diagonal folds to form a diamond. Turn over and repeat this step on the back to make the shape shown in diagram 2.

3 Fold the top flap on the right over to the left. Turn the paper over and repeat, folding the top right flap only to the left.

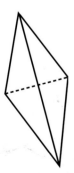

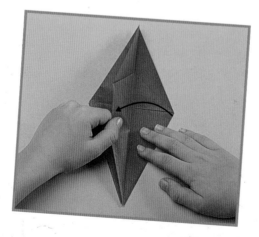

diagram 2

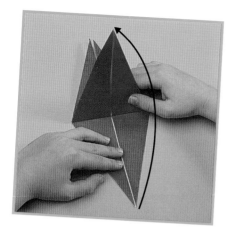

Fold the bottom flap up. Turn over and repeat.

5

Pull the hidden points in the middle out and down, and crease them in the position shown. These will make the bird's head and tail.

6

Fold the head down as shown, unfold it then make an internal reverse fold as shown at the top of page 111. To make your bird flap its wings, hold the two bottom points and gently pull them apart.

FURTHER IDEAS

Make birds in different sizes and colours, attach thread to their bodies and hang them from a coat hanger to make a mobile.

Blow-up Box

This classic Japanese origami design just looks like an interesting shape when you have finished folding it. However, if you blow into it, it inflates to make a three-dimensional box. Fold the Rocket Base first, and with a few simple folds and some clever tucks, you will soon have an origami shape with a built-in surprise!

1 Begin with the Rocket Base. Fold the bottom corners of the two front flaps up to the top point.

2 Turn the paper over and repeat on the other side.

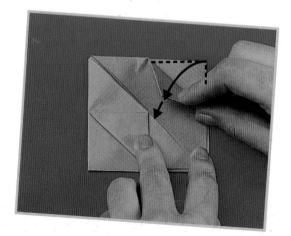

3 Bring the two outer corners of the front flaps in to the centre and crease as shown.

4

Turn the
paper over
and repeat.

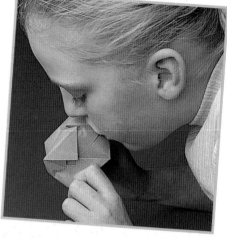

5

Make sure the loose
points are at the top
and tuck the front two
loose points in the
triangle pockets as far
as you can. They will
not go all the way in.
Turn the paper over
and repeat.

Top

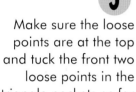

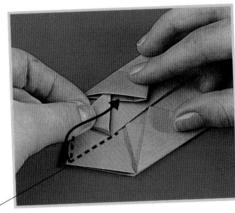

6

Hold the paper lightly
between your fingers and
thumbs. Put the open end
to your mouth and blow
into the opening. The box
should now inflate.

FURTHER IDEAS

Make boxes in bright
metallic colours and
hang them up as
Christmas decorations,
or make red lanterns
for Chinese New Year.

Handmade Cards by Tamsin Carter

Commercial greetings cards are sent for all sorts of reasons: to wish someone a happy birthday, or good luck; to celebrate a festival such as Christmas or New Year; to say thank you, congratulations, or just hello. A greetings card tells someone that you are thinking of them and that you care, and it gives them a picture to display in their home. Just think how much more special a handmade card is, because you have created it yourself and chosen the message personally.

People all over the world have been sending each other hand-decorated messages and cards for hundreds of years, probably since paper became widely available. The oldest known Valentine's card was made in the 1400s and is in the British Museum. Printed cards came later, in the nineteenth century, and were mainly for celebrating holidays or religious festivals.

In this section I show you how to make a variety of different cards using a range of materials including felt, pipe cleaners, beads and even wobbly plastic eyes! Do not worry if you think you cannot draw very well, as there are patterns in the back of the book to help you. I have also included a section on page 156 which shows you easy methods of transferring designs and scoring and folding card. There are lots of fun techniques to try like paint spattering, sewing and collage.

Inspiration can come from all sorts of sources. I usually think of the person I am making the card for, and that gets me started. In this book there are cards inspired by space, nature, musical instruments, dinosaurs, sport, famous artists and ancient wonders. Once you have chosen your subject, you can investigate it further by searching for information in libraries, galleries and museums and on the internet.

Nature is a very good place to find inspiration. You can collect leaves, sticks and flowers to make a collage, or look at the weather and the amazing effects it has on our world. Sometimes the materials themselves can be inspiring: just laying them out in front of you can be enough to trigger an idea and get you started.

Most importantly remember there are no rules; the more you experiment and dare to try something new, the more wonderful your cards will be. A card can be simple or complicated, take an hour to make or just five minutes. A greetings card is very special, it is a gift and a message all in one. Enjoy making them and people will enjoy receiving them.

Greetings cards first became really popular in Victorian times. This beautifully painted nineteenth century Christmas card shows the ornate and detailed style typical of the Victorians.

Nazca Birds

In the 1930s, pilots were flying over the desert in Peru in South America when they saw giant drawings on the ground. There was a monkey the size of a football pitch, a lizard twice that length, a spider, fish, birds and insects. It is thought that they were made by the Nazca Indians around two thousand years ago, but nobody knows why. Have a look at them in a library or on the internet and try to imagine why they were made and how. This card is inspired by one of the Nazca drawings, of a large bird called a condor.

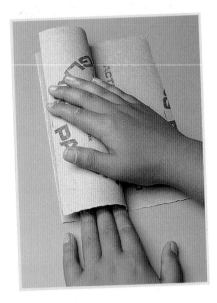

! Ask an adult to help you to photocopy the design.

2 Photocopy the design on page 158. Cut round it roughly and stick it on to the folded sandpaper with a glue stick. Make sure that the dotted line that runs down one side of the pattern is up against the outer folds. Don't worry if the bird's wings overlap the edge.

1 Fold a sheet of A4 fine sandpaper in half with the sand on the outside. Then fold the top layer in half again, back towards the centre fold. Turn the sandpaper over and fold the top layer in half as before so that you have four equal layers.

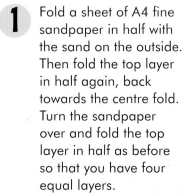

3 Carefully cut out the bird shape. Make sure you do not cut off the ends of the feathers that have dotted lines. They should extend to meet the fold.

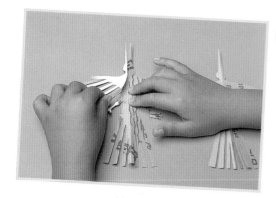

4 Open out the sandpaper to reveal two condors joined at the wings. Peel off the photocopied pattern. Do not worry if some parts will not peel off – they will not show.

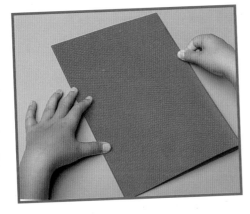

5 Score and fold a piece of A3 corrugated card in half widthways to make a card (see page 156).

6 Stick the condors on to the card with strong, clear glue.

FURTHER IDEAS
Invent your own fold-out Nazca style designs, using geometric shapes, straight lines and repeated patterns.

Fantasy Planets

Space ... the final frontier! What is out there? We know about the planets in our own solar system, but we cannot be sure about what lies beyond. Many people are fascinated by space and all the unanswered questions we have about the universe. With space, you can let your imagination run wild! In this project, spattering white paint on black card makes the perfect starry background for your own fantasy solar system. You can create all kinds of weird and wonderful planets using paint techniques and metallic pens.

YOU WILL NEED
Thick black card
Coloured card • Paints
Metallic pens • Pencil
Empty ballpoint pen • Ruler
Sponge • Toothbrush
Scissors • Compasses

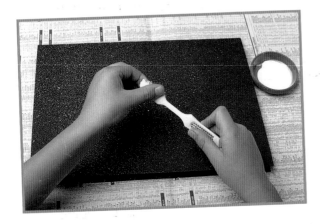

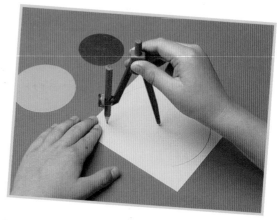

1 Score and fold a large piece of black card in half. Dip the end of a toothbrush in some white paint and slowly run your finger over the bristles so the paint spatters onto the card. Allow to dry. You can spatter on a second colour if you like.

Note Practise spattering or sponging on scrap paper first, and always cover your work surface.

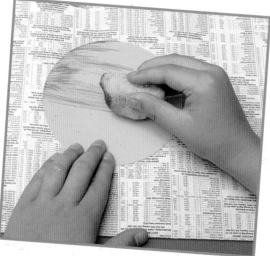

2 To make the planets, use compasses to draw four different sized circles on coloured card. Cut them out.

3 Put a circle on some newspaper. Dip a sponge in paint and lightly stroke the colour a little way across from one side. Stroking in a slight curve will make the planet look three-dimensional.

4

Sponge another colour across from the other side and then spatter more colours over the top with the toothbrush. Experiment with sponging, spattering and using metallic pens to decorate the other planets. Leave to dry.

5

Using the pattern on page 157 as a guide, draw a planet ring on card. Make sure it will fit over one of your planets. Then cut it out and lightly sponge some paint across it. Leave it to dry.

6 Slip the ring over a planet. Move the planets around on your space background until you are happy with the picture. Then stick them all in place with glue.

FURTHER IDEAS
Add aliens, rockets, meteors or space ships to your fantasy solar system.

Matisse Collage

Henri Matisse was a famous artist. He was influenced by many different styles. Once when Matisse was ill, he found it difficult to paint, so he made pictures by cutting shapes out of paper and sticking them down to make a collage. 'I am drawing directly in colour,' he said.

In this project I show you how to make a collage inspired by Matisse. There is a pattern on page 158 to help you, but if you feel confident, you could try cutting out your own picture freehand as Matisse did.

YOU WILL NEED
Thin card • Thick card
Compasses • Scissors
Empty ballpoint pen • Ruler
Glue stick • Pencil • Paper
Masking tape

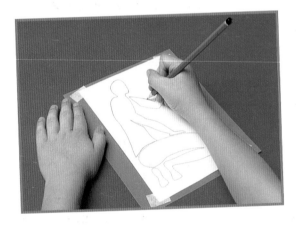

1 Transfer the pattern on page 158 on to thin card, or draw it freehand if you prefer.

2 On a different coloured piece of card, draw or transfer the plant design. Then, using compasses, draw a circle roughly 25mm (1in) across.

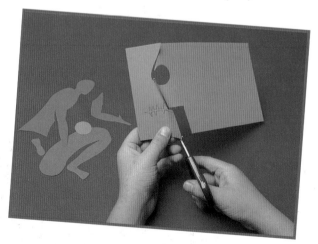

3 Cut out all of the shapes using scissors.

 4

Take an A5 piece of thin card and trim 5–10mm (¼in) off each side. Try to leave an uneven edge as you cut.

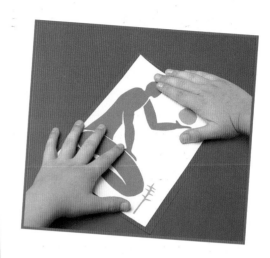

5

Arrange the pieces on the card, leaving small gaps in the figure as shown. Glue them in place with a glue stick.

 6

Score and fold a piece of A4 card in half and stick the finished collage on to the front.

FURTHER IDEAS
Cut out the shapes for figures, animals or plants, to make your own original collages.

It's a Goal!

Soccer is a brilliant game to play and to watch. Its history dates as far back as the ancient Chinese, Greek, Mayan and Egyptian societies. Modern football developed from games played in England in the nineteenth century. In 1863 these games were separated into rugby football, which is where American football comes from, and Association football, or soccer. You can make this soccer goal card by sewing the net with coloured thread, attaching the goal posts and finally putting the ball in the net – one-nil!

YOU WILL NEED
Thick card • Thin card
Strong, clear glue • Glue stick
Blunt-ended needle • Scissors
Masking tape • Pencil • Paper
Thick corrugated cardboard
Thick coloured thread
Compasses • Black pen

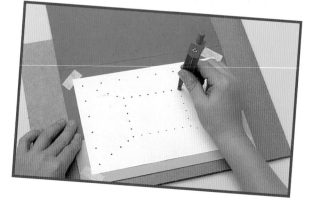

1 Score and fold a piece of thick A4 card in half. Stick a strip of green paper across the bottom.

2 Photocopy the dot pattern on page 159 and secure it to the front of the card with masking tape. Open the card and lay the front over a piece of thick corrugated cardboard to protect your work surface. Using the point of your compasses, pierce holes through the dots on the pattern. Then remove the pattern.

> (!) Ask an adult to help you to photocopy the design.

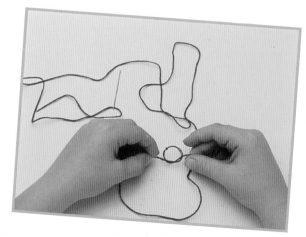

3 Thread one end of a long piece of coloured thread through the eye of a blunt-ended needle. Tie a large knot in the other end.

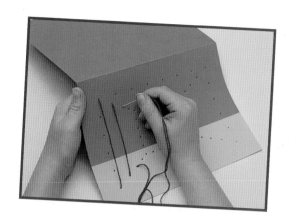

Push the needle up through the hole in the bottom left-hand corner and down through the hole in the top left-hand corner. Do the same for the next holes and continue until all the vertical lines are sewn.

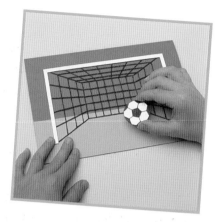

5

Now sew all the other lines of the net, as shown. You will use some holes more than once. If you run out of thread, tie a knot and thread your needle again.

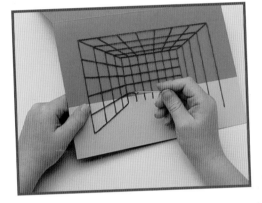

6 Transfer the goal posts and the football design on page 159 on to white card and cut them out. Colour the football with a black pen as shown. Use strong, clear glue to stick the goal posts and ball on to the card.

FURTHER IDEAS
Sew a basketball hoop, tennis racket, spider's web or even somebody's name to make an unusual card.

Spooky Wood

Woods can be very spooky at night. It is easy to imagine pairs of eyes peeping out from the dark. Woods and forests are often used to conjure up a spooky atmosphere in paintings, stories, poems and films. Collect interesting looking sticks and twigs to make the trees in this spooky wood card. Imagine the different creatures that live in the wood as you stick on their eyes. You could even write a spooky poem in the card.

YOU WILL NEED

Bright corrugated card • Thick card
Empty ballpoint pen • Ruler
Scissors • Plastic eyes
Masking tape • Pencil • Paper
Sticks • Strong, clear glue
Black felt

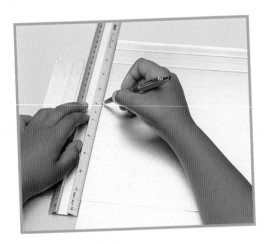

1 Enlarge the design on page 159 on a photocopier and transfer it on to the back of a piece of bright corrugated card. Enlarge the design by 141% to fit on to a sheet of A4, or by 200%, to fit on to a sheet of A3. Cut it out and score and fold along the dotted lines.

Ask an adult to help you to photocopy the design.

2 Fold up the left-hand side of the corrugated card to make a rectangular tube. Squeeze a line of strong, clear glue on to the corrugated side of the end tab and stick it in place. Do the same on the right, but leave the top and bottom open.

3 Measure the flat area left in the middle. Cut out a piece of black felt the same size. Stick it on with strong, clear glue.

4 Trim the sticks so they fit roughly inside the flat area. Then arrange them on top of the felt to look like a wood.

Ask an adult to help you to cut the sticks.

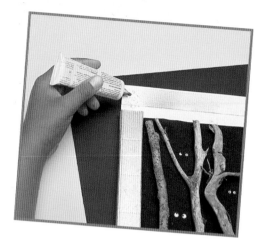

5

When you are happy with the picture, glue down the sticks with strong, clear glue. Then stick pairs of plastic eyes in between the sticks. Leave to dry.

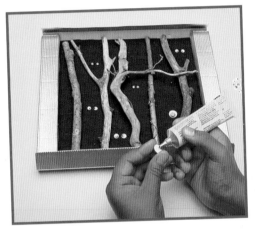

6

Finish the frame by gluing the corners of the top and bottom flaps and sticking them down. Finally stick the finished frame on to a piece of folded card.

FURTHER IDEAS
Spray sticks with snow spray or silver paint and add a silvery moon to make a winter scene.

Funky Fish

Fish are very beautiful. It is amazing how many different shapes and colours there are. We have only explored one hundredth of the seabeds on our planet, so there may be even more weird and wonderful varieties of fish to be discovered in the future. In this project, fish are threaded on to metallic thread with beads, to make a bubbly underwater scene.

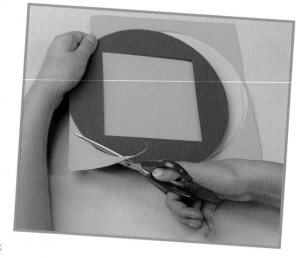

1 Score and fold a large piece of thick card in half. Using compasses and a pencil, draw a circle overlapping the fold and the bottom by about 5mm (¼in) as shown. Cut it out.

2 Open the circular card and draw a square on the front. Cut out the square to make a window. Stick a piece of coloured paper on the inside back of the card (the side you can see through the window) and trim to size.

3 Fold three small pieces of thin coloured card in half. Transfer one of the fish designs on page 157 on to each piece of card. Cut out the fish – you will end up with two of each design.

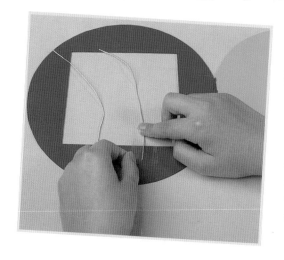

4

Lay two pieces of metallic thread over the window on the inside of the card. Secure them at the bottom with sticky tape.

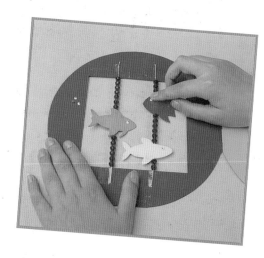

5

Thread some beads on to the first piece of metallic thread. Then take a pair of fish and put glue on one of them. Stick the fish together, sandwiching the thread between them as shown.

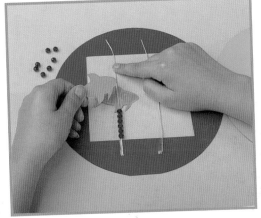

6

Thread on more beads and secure the top of the thread with sticky tape. Do the same on the other thread, using more beads and the other two fish. Finally stick plastic eyes on both sides of the fish using strong, clear glue.

FURTHER IDEAS

Make a card with a different shaped window. Add other sea creatures – an octopus, seahorse or dolphin.

Smiling Sunflower

Flowers are often used to cheer people up, and for special occasions like Mother's day and Valentine's day. Different flowers can mean different things. Red flowers are usually for love – roses, carnations and tulips. White flowers such as daisies and lilies represent innocence and purity. Pansies and poppies are for remembrance, sweet peas for goodbyes, and forget-me-nots speak for themselves! Sunflowers turn their heads to follow the sun across the sky. This one has a lovely smile and a stem made from flexible pipe cleaners, so that its head bobs cheerfully when it moves.

YOU WILL NEED
Card • Pipe cleaners
Scissors • Ruler • Pen
Plastic eyes • Pencil
Masking tape • Paper
Compasses • Eraser • Felt
Empty ballpoint pen
Strong, clear glue

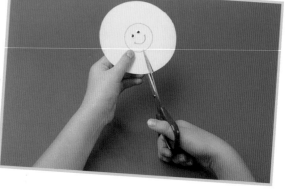

2 Cut a slit from the edge up to the small circle. Then cut a second slit next to it. Continue all of the way around the face. Carefully erase the pencil circle.

1 Use compasses and a pencil to draw a large circle on some yellow card, then cut it out. Draw a smaller circle in the middle for the sunflower's face. Stick on plastic eyes using strong, clear glue, and draw on a smile.

3 Fold every other petal away from you until there is a space between each one. Then hold all the folded petals together and wrap the end of a pipe cleaner round them until they are secure. The rest of this pipe cleaner will be the sunflower's stem.

Twist more pipe cleaners around the stem to make it longer and thicker. Cut two sets of leaves out of felt. Push the leaves between the pipe cleaners as shown.

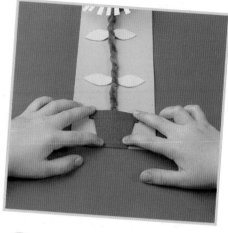

5

Transfer the pattern for the flower pot on page 157 on to card. Cut it out. Score along the dotted lines as shown and fold back the tabs.

6 Score and fold a piece of A4 size card in half lengthways. Glue the bottom half of the flower stem to the card. Put glue on the flower pot tabs and stick the pot over the stem.

FURTHER IDEAS
Create flowers using textured papers or metallic card. Try making several layers of petals.

Pop-up Dinosaur

Millions of years ago there were no people, and dinosaurs ruled the earth. We know from digging up their bones what kinds of dinosaurs existed, their sizes and shapes and even what they ate. But we do not know what colours they were. So when you make this pop-up dinosaur card, imagine the colours for yourself and create a prehistoric world of your own. There are patterns for the Tyrannosaurus Rex and the Pteranodon in the back of the book, but you could draw any of your favourite dinosaurs – or even invent your own.

YOU WILL NEED

Thick card • Scissors
Coloured and metallic paint pens
Strong, clear glue • Pencil
Ruler • Masking tape • Paper
Thin black pen • Acrylic paint
Natural sponge

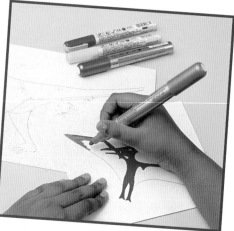

 Transfer the Tyrannosaurus Rex and Pteranodon designs on page 158 on to thick card. Colour them in using paint pens.

 Score and fold a large piece of thick card in half. On the top half of the inside, sponge on a strip of paint to suggest a landscape. Leave to dry.

Note Sponging two similar colours on top of each other can make a landscape look more realistic.

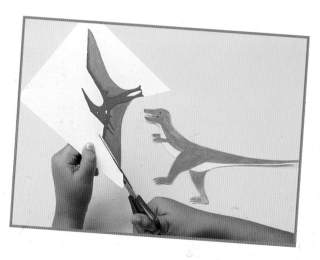

3 Draw the outlines and the eyes with a thin black pen. Carefully cut the dinosaurs out. If some areas are difficult to cut out, colour them black so that they will not show up.

Decide where you want your dinosaur to stand, and mark the spot lightly with a pencil. Fold the card inside out. From the fold side, cut two slits up to the mark you have made.

Open up the card and press between the cuts to push out a tab. Then close the card again with the tab pushed out and press. This will help to fold the tab in the right position.

Open the card and stick the Tyrannosaurus's leg on to the tab with strong, clear glue. Glue the Pteranodon on to the background.

Note To make the Pteranodon stand out from the card, stick a little pad of folded card on the back before gluing it in place.

FURTHER IDEAS
Make pop-up scenery for your dinosaur world: hills, trees, plants, mountains — even a volcano!

Jazzy Guitar

Guitars are played all over the world to make all kinds of music – from Spanish flamenco and folk music to pop, rock and jazz. They usually have six strings, although there are twelve-string guitars as well. The strings play a different note depending on how taut they are. They can be adjusted to the right pitch using a special tuning key. You can make a card in the shape of a guitar and add strings made from coloured thread.

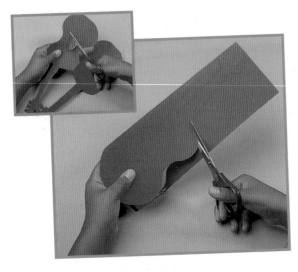

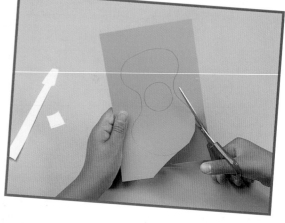

1 Score and fold a piece of thick coloured card in half and transfer the outer guitar design on page 157 on to it. Make sure that the dotted edges marked on the pattern go over the fold line. Cut out the guitar. Open the card and cut out the circle in the middle from the front of the card only.

2 Transfer the inner guitar pattern and the neck and soundboard patterns on to coloured card and cut them out.

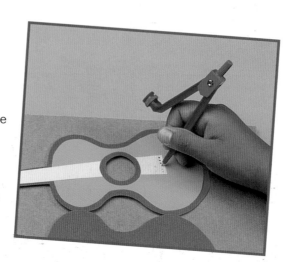

3 Stick the inner guitar, neck and soundboard on to the card. Open up the card, then place it over some thick corrugated cardboard. Pierce the sets of holes on the neck and the soundboard with compasses.

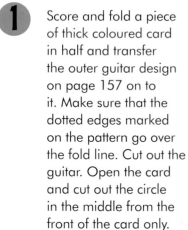

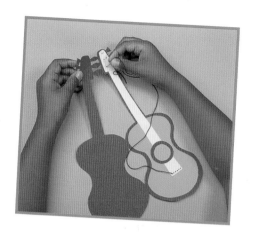

4 Thread one end of a piece of coloured thread through the eye of a blunt-ended needle and tie a knot in the other end. Sew up through the far left hole at the bottom and down through the far left hole at the top.

5 Gently pull the thread through until taut. Do not pull it too tight, or the card will bend. Then wrap the end round the bottom left tuning key and tie a knot. Repeat for the other five strings.

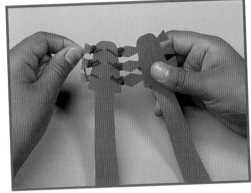

6 Decorate your guitar by drawing big dots around the edge with a paint pen.

Note If you find knotting the thread difficult, you can tape the loose ends at the back.

FURTHER IDEAS
Try making other musical instruments. A banjo has five strings, a double bass has four and a harp has lots and lots.

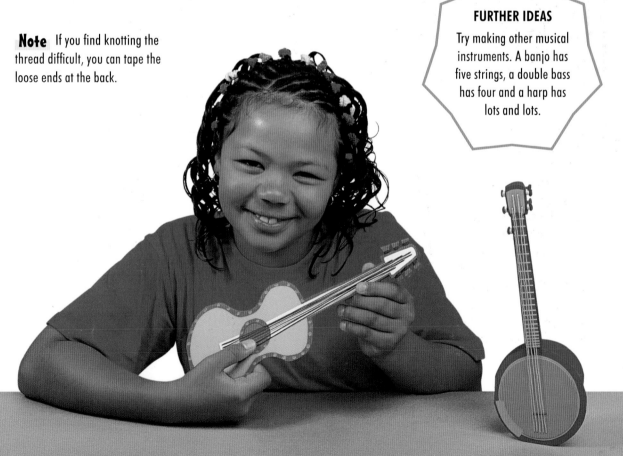

Winter Window

Many cultures around the world have a winter festival. Most of them are linked to the winter solstice. This is the time of the shortest day and the longest night of the year. Some of the festivals celebrated during winter are Christmas, Bodhi Day, Hanukkah and Yule. Winter is a lovely time to gather with family and friends and stay warm by the fire. You can make a winter window card using polystyrene balls for snow and a clear plastic bag such as a sandwich or freezer bag for the window.

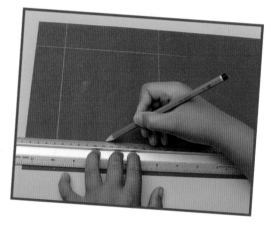

Cut out two pieces of card, one 42cm x 21cm (16½in x 8¼in), and one 21cm (8¼in) square. Fold the big one in half.

On the inside front of the folded card, measure 4cm (1½in) in from each side and draw lines to make a square. Cut out the square.

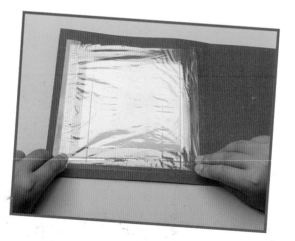

Open up the card again and lay a clear sandwich bag over the square. You may need to trim the top of the bag to fit. Use sticky tape to stick it on at the bottom and sides. Do not stretch the bag too tightly, as this will warp the card.

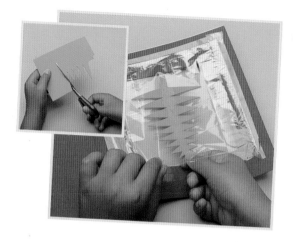

4

Draw a tree on high-density foam and cut it out. Put a line of glue down the middle of the tree and stick it inside the bag. Make sure the glued side of the tree is uppermost.

5

Sprinkle some polystyrene balls in to the bag and tape up the top.

6

Spread strong, clear glue on the inside of the card window frame. Stick the square piece of card on top.

FURTHER IDEAS

You can make all sorts of things to stand in your snow storm — try a snowman, a house, a reindeer or a penguin.

Techniques

Ask an adult to help you to photocopy the patterns.

Transferring a design

You can photocopy the patterns on pages 157–159 and transfer them on to card using the technique shown below. Use the photocopier to enlarge or reduce the designs if you need to.

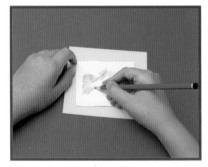 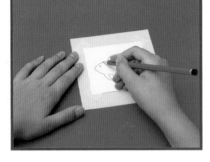 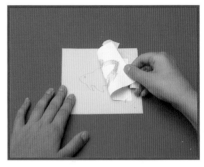

1 Photocopy the design. Turn over the photocopy and scribble over the lines with a soft pencil.

2 Turn the photocopy over and tape it to your card using masking tape. Then go over the lines of the design with a pencil.

3 Peel back the photocopy to reveal the transferred design.

Scoring and folding card

Dotted lines on the patterns need to be scored and folded. You can also use scoring to help make neat cards. Find the centre line by measuring the halfway point and score and fold as shown below.

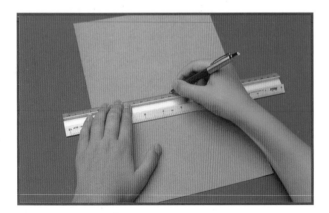 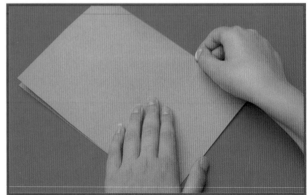

1 Score a line across the middle of the card with a ballpoint pen that has run out of ink.

2 Fold the card and run the back of your fingernail along the fold to press it down. If the edges are not exactly square, you can trim them with scissors.

Patterns

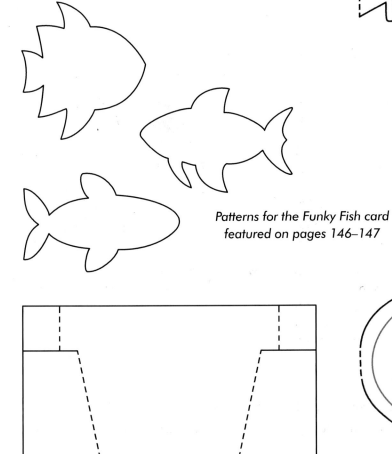

Patterns for the Funky Fish card
featured on pages 146–147

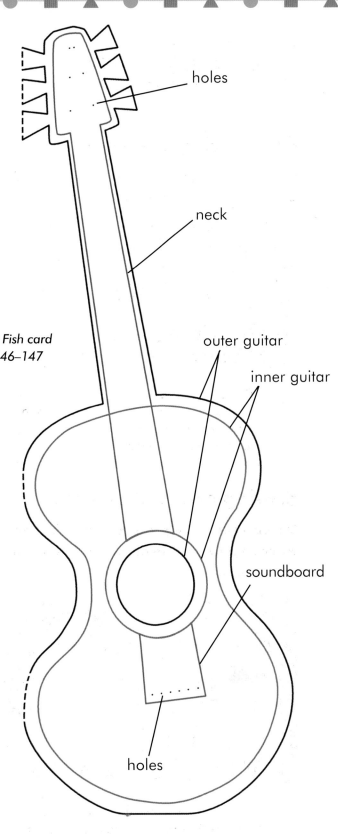

holes

neck

outer guitar

inner guitar

soundboard

holes

Pattern for the flower pot in the Smiling
Sunflower card featured on pages 148–149

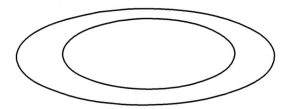

Pattern for the planet ring used in the Fantasy
Planets card featured on pages 138–139

Pattern for the Jazzy Guitar card featured
on pages 152–153

Pattern for the Matisse
Collage card featured on
pages 140–141

Pattern for the Nazca
Birds card featured on
pages 136–137

Patterns for the Pop-up Dinosaur card
featured on pages 150–151

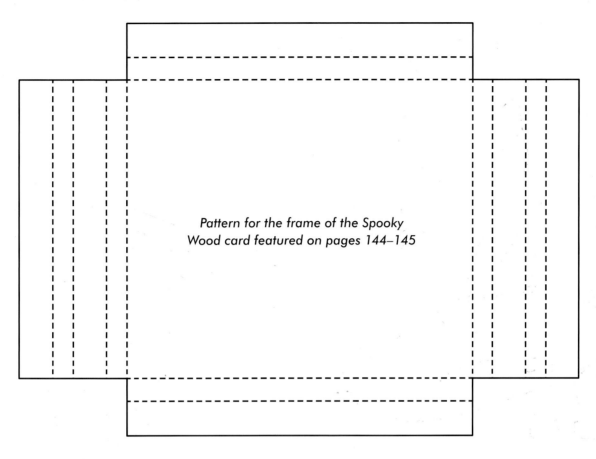

*Pattern for the frame of the Spooky
Wood card featured on pages 144–145*

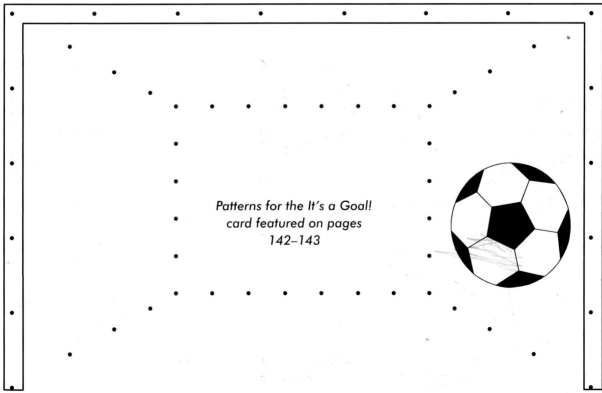

*Patterns for the It's a Goal!
card featured on pages
142–143*

About the authors

Judy Balchin studied art at Cardiff College of Art and then specialized in graphic design at Kent Institute of Art and Design. She now designs craft kits for both adults and children, and runs workshops for all ages. Judy has appeared on television as a craft demonstrator and her craft techniques have been featured in three videos. She frequently writes articles for art and craft magazines.

Michelle Powell studied art and design at Bath College of Higher Education. She majored in paper making and graduated with a degree in teaching art. A crafter at heart, Michelle has a passion for paper, beads and fabric and has crafted as long as she can remember. She has worked as a craft product designer and magazine contributor, prior to becoming editor of *Scrapbook Magic* and *Practical Crafts*. Michelle is now a craft designer and author.

Tamsin Carter studied graphic design at Kingsway College, London. She was a book designer for a number of years and now runs a successful book, graphic and web design business, Pynto Ltd. She enjoys many crafts, most recently using beads, foam and wire as well as silver clay and jewellery making. She always makes the special people in her life handmade cards and really enjoys making each one different. She lives in Devon with her husband, Steve, two children and three cats.

Clive Stevens studied art and design in Canada, where he then worked as a graphic designer, art director and illustrator. He ran his own advertising agency in the UK for 20 years. Clive has written four books on paperfolding and paper sculpture. He has run weekend courses in paper sculpture and written articles on paperfolding techniques for *Crafts Magazine* and *The Artist*. He has also produced paper sculpture animations for television advertising. He presently creates paper sculptures for sale throughout the world, and travels around British schools demonstrating paper crafts.